BeagleBone for Secret Agents

Browse anonymously, communicate secretly, and create
custom security solutions with open source software,
the BeagleBone Black, and cryptographic hardware

Josh Datko

[PACKT] open source ✳
PUBLISHING   community experience distilled

BIRMINGHAM - MUMBAI

BeagleBone for Secret Agents

Copyright © 2014 Packt Publishing

First published: September 2014

Production reference: 1190914

Published by Packt Publishing Ltd.
Livery Place
35 Livery Street
Birmingham B3 2PB, UK.

ISBN 978-1-78398-604-0

www.packtpub.com

Cover image by Pratyush Mohanta (tysoncinematics@gmail.com)

Credits

Author
Josh Datko

Reviewers
Raymond Boswel

Dr. Philip Polstra

Norbert Varga

Jay Zarfoss

Commissioning Editor
Akram Hussain

Acquisition Editor
Greg Wild

Content Development Editor
Dayan Hyames

Technical Editors
Taabish Khan

Humera Shaikh

Copy Editors
Dipti Kapadia

Laxmi Subramanian

Project Coordinator
Venitha Cutinho

Proofreader
Ameesha Green

Indexers
Priya Sane

Tejal Soni

Graphics
Ronak Dhruv

Valentına D'silva

Production Coordinator
Saiprasad Kadam

Cover Work
Saiprasad Kadam

Foreword

The number of things on the Internet of Things is growing at an unfathomable rate. A thermostat, weather station, desk lamp, and car charger are devices designed to be as unobtrusive as possible. At the same time, we demand that they be knowledgeable about our daily lives and quickly respond to our daily wants and needs. As technology becomes more powerful and more pervasive, we don't spend much time thinking about security. It's a common misconception: security is for my passwords and my browser, so why does my electric meter need it? It is this type of gap in consideration that can undermine the usability of the things we use every day.

I recently built an interactive exhibit at a museum. In order to monitor the use and to know when maintenance was needed, I had the exhibit report of various interaction events to the Internet, where I could see and monitor it. Security is for my bank account; I didn't need to encrypt these messages! I simply needed to get my data from point A to point B, so I used a clear-text method for posting to a database. Who cares if a man-in-the-middle attack is possible? Who cares if someone does a replay attack and posts the same data twice to my database? If other people saw the data being passed back and forth, I figured I was doing something pretty cool because people generally don't care about event flags. This changed when I had a discussion with someone who had a reason to believe that the global temperature data was being modified for various political and financial reasons. It suddenly struck me that if we're going to make unbiased scientific decisions on (pick your societal ill), then we need data that we can rely on. Cryptography is not always about secrets; it's also about ensuring that you are having the conversation you want to have with the person you want to talk to.

We are riding on a wave of great creativity and exploration within physical computing that will increase the quality of our relationship with technology and our quality of life. Most people don't think of these devices as needing cryptography, but when left without thought, the Internet of Things can wreak more havoc than identity theft or wire fraud. This is not about spying, hackers, or rogue governments. If we can push technology towards a more secure means of communication, we ensure the freedom that modern society takes for granted. We should be laying the groundwork today for the future generation of hackers, makers, tinkerers, and innovators to create amazing things for sure—but we should be building this groundwork with security in mind.

Over the past few months, I have begun to learn about hashes, HMACs, and nonces. Cryptography is no longer restricted to the realm of applied math PhDs or government-funded researchers. It has been made approachable and stronger by a loose net of enthusiasts that take it upon themselves to be the quiet but persistent force of change. I encourage you to become an educated participant in the modern world of technology. Cryptography should not be simply seen as something to strengthen a project. Rather, we must reinforce a trend of secure communication so that future projects and technologies use proper encryption and cryptography without thinking about it.

Josh came to SparkFun as part of our Hacker-in-Residence program. We worked with him to build his vision—a module that would help fellow hackers secure their projects. I hope that you will find this book, which contains projects that combine electronics, software, and security, of interest. It will make you appreciate the challenge and necessity of securing our Internet of Things.

Nathan Seidle
CEO, SparkFun Electronics

About the Author

Josh Datko is the founder of Cryptotronix, LLC, an open source hardware company that specializes in embedded, cryptographic electronics. He graduated with distinction from the US Naval Academy with a Bachelor's of Science in Computer Science and then served 10 years in the Navy, both actively and as a reserve submarine officer. He has been deployed to locations worldwide including Afghanistan in support of Operation Enduring Freedom. In 2014, Josh presented at both the HOPE and DEF CON conferences. He completed his Master's of Science in Computer Science, with a focus on security and networking, from Drexel University.

I'd like to thank F. and A. for their love and support.

About the Reviewers

Raymond Boswel is an electronic engineer from South Africa. He works as a systems engineer for a telecommunications company. Although the powers that be don't condone playing around with single-board computers during office hours, he enjoys fiddling with them during his free time. So far, he's used his Beagle for convolutional, frequency-response modeling to spice up his guitar amplifier, automation, and time-lapse photography. Having read this book, he might just turn his attention to espionage. Enjoy!

Dr. Philip Polstra (known as Dr. Phil to his friends) is an internationally recognized hardware hacker. His work has been presented at numerous conferences around the globe, including repeat performances at DEFCON, Black Hat, 44CON, Maker Faire, and other top conferences. He is a well-known expert on USB Forensics and has published several articles on this topic.

Recently, Dr. Polstra has developed a penetration testing Linux distribution, known as The Deck, for the BeagleBone and BeagleBoard family of small computer boards. He has also developed a new way of doing penetration testing with multiple low-power devices, including an aerial hacking drone. This work is described in his book *Hacking and Penetration Testing With Low Power Devices, Syngress*. He has also been a technical reviewer on several books including *BeagleBone Home Automation, Packt Publishing*.

Dr. Polstra is an Associate Professor at Bloomsburg University of Pennsylvania (http://bloomu.edu/digital_forensics), where he teaches Digital Forensics among other topics. In addition to teaching, he provides training and performs penetration tests on a consulting basis. When he is not working, he has been known to fly and build aircrafts and tinker with electronics. His latest happenings can be found on his blog at http://polstra.org. You can also follow him @ppolstra on Twitter.

Norbert Varga has over 5 years of experience in the software and hardware development industry. He is responsible for embedded software development, hardware-software integration, and wireless telecommunication solutions for his current employer, BME-Infokom.

He has extensive experience in networking and hardware-software integration — he has engineered advanced systems including wireless mesh networks and smart metering solutions. He also has a strong background in Linux system administration and software development.

Previously, Norbert has worked as a software developer on various projects at the Budapest University of Technology and Economics (Department of Telecommunications), which is the most renowned technical university in Hungary. He has played a key role throughout all the development processes, ranging from initial planning through implementation to testing and production support.

He has a personal blog where he writes about his current projects at `http://nonoo.hu/`.

Jay Zarfoss is a senior cloud security engineer at Netflix, where he is responsible for building secure software solutions in Amazon Cloud. He has over 10 years of experience in various fields of computer security in both public and private sectors, and he has a broad range of eclectic interests in the realm of computer security, such as tracking down and studying Botnets, applying cryptography to real-life situations, and building security and key management solutions for virtualized environments. When not implementing a timing attack or learning a foreign language, Jay enjoys the outdoors with his wife Stefanie.

www.PacktPub.com

Support files, eBooks, discount offers, and more

You might want to visit www.PacktPub.com for support files and downloads related to your book.

Did you know that Packt offers eBook versions of every book published, with PDF and ePub files available? You can upgrade to the eBook version at www.PacktPub.com and as a print book customer, you are entitled to a discount on the eBook copy. Get in touch with us at service@packtpub.com for more details.

At www.PacktPub.com, you can also read a collection of free technical articles, sign up for a range of free newsletters and receive exclusive discounts and offers on Packt books and eBooks.

http://PacktLib.PacktPub.com

Do you need instant solutions to your IT questions? PacktLib is Packt's online digital book library. Here, you can access, read and search across Packt's entire library of books.

Why subscribe?

- Fully searchable across every book published by Packt
- Copy and paste, print and bookmark content
- On demand and accessible via web browser

Free access for Packt account holders

If you have an account with Packt at www.PacktPub.com, you can use this to access PacktLib today and view nine entirely free books. Simply use your login credentials for immediate access.

Table of Contents

Preface

BeagleBone Black inspires embedded hackers in different ways. Some see it as a controller board for a small robot, while others see it as a low-power, network server. In this book, we'll treat BeagleBone Black as a defender of personal security and privacy. Each chapter will discuss a technology and then provide a project to reinforce the concept.

Let's get started!

What this book covers

Chapter 1, Creating Your BeagleBone Black Development Environment, starts the journey by showing you how to set up Emacs to maximize your embedded hacking.

Chapter 2, Circumventing Censorship with a Tor Bridge, walks through how to transform the BeagleBone Black into a Tor server with a front panel interface.

Chapter 3, Adding Hardware Security with the CryptoCape, investigates biometric authentication and specialized security chips.

Chapter 4, Protecting GPG Keys with a Trusted Platform Module, shows you how to use the BeagleBone Black to safeguard e-mail encryption keys.

Chapter 5, Chatting Off-the-Record, details how to run an IRC gateway on the BeagleBone Black to encrypt instant messaging.

Appendix, Selected Bibliography, lists the referenced works cited throughout the book.

What you need for this book

This book contains several independent projects that use various software packages and hardware components. All the software is open source, and installation instructions are given throughout the chapter. A list of all the necessary hardware is maintained as a SparkFun Electronics wish list at https://www.sparkfun.com/ wish_lists/93119. Each chapter will list the required components for that project, so it's best to first read the chapter and then collect the necessary hardware.

Who this book is for

If you have an interest in individual security and privacy on the Internet, then you hopefully should enjoy this book. If you have a security background but are new to embedded computing, then you should find the projects challenging but rewarding. Conversely, if you are versed in electronics and are working with GNU/Linux distributions but haven't studied the security technologies mentioned in this book, then you should appreciate the discussions of the technologies in each chapter.

Conventions

In this book, you will find a number of styles of text that distinguish between different kinds of information. Here are some examples of these styles and an explanation of their meaning.

Code words in text, database table names, folder names, filenames, file extensions, pathnames, dummy URLs, user input, and Twitter handles are shown as follows: "The LCD, controlled by the FrontPanelDisplay class, writes to the serial port, /dev/ttyO4, on BBB's UART 4 at 9600 baud."

A block of code is set as follows:

```
self.clear_screen()
up_str = '{0:<16}'.format('Up:    ' + self.block_char * up)
dn_str = '{0:<16}'.format('Down: ' + self.block_char * down)

self.port.write(up_str)
self.port.write(dn_str)
```

When we wish to draw your attention to a particular part of a code block, the relevant lines or items are set in bold:

```
import Adafruit_BBIO.UART as UART
import serial
class FrontPanelDisplay(object):
```

```
def __init__(self):
    self.uart = 'UART4'
    UART.setup(self.uart)
    self.port = serial.Serial(port="/dev/ttyO4", baudrate=9600)
    self.port.open()
```

Any command-line input or output is written as follows:

```
Mar 25 21:37:43.000 [notice] Tor has successfully opened a circuit. Looks
like client functionality is working.
Mar 25 21:37:43.000 [notice] Bootstrapped 100%: Done.
```

New terms and **important words** are shown in bold. Words that you see on the screen, in menus or dialog boxes for example, appear in the text like this: "To connect to your bridge, launch the Tor browser and click on **Open Settings** as it starts up."

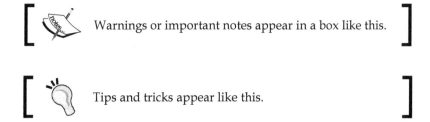

Warnings or important notes appear in a box like this.

Tips and tricks appear like this.

Reader feedback

Feedback from our readers is always welcome. Let us know what you think about this book—what you liked or may have disliked. Reader feedback is important for us to develop titles that you really get the most out of.

To send us general feedback, simply send an e-mail to feedback@packtpub.com, and mention the book title via the subject of your message. If there is a topic that you have expertise in and you are interested in either writing or contributing to a book, see our author guide on www.packtpub.com/authors.

Customer support

Now that you are the proud owner of a Packt book, we have a number of things to help you to get the most from your purchase.

Downloading the example code

You can download the example code files for all Packt books you have purchased from your account at `http://www.packtpub.com`. If you purchased this book elsewhere, you can visit `http://www.packtpub.com/support` and register to have the files e-mailed directly to you.

Errata

Although we have taken every care to ensure the accuracy of our content, mistakes do happen. If you find a mistake in one of our books — maybe a mistake in the text or the code — we would be grateful if you would report this to us. By doing so, you can save other readers from frustration and help us improve subsequent versions of this book. If you find any errata, please report them by visiting `http://www.packtpub.com/submit-errata`, selecting your book, clicking on the **errata submission form** link, and entering the details of your errata. Once your errata are verified, your submission will be accepted and the errata will be uploaded on our website, or added to any list of existing errata, under the Errata section of that title. Any existing errata can be viewed by selecting your title from `http://www.packtpub.com/support`.

Piracy

Piracy of copyright material on the Internet is an ongoing problem across all media. At Packt, we take the protection of our copyright and licenses very seriously. If you come across any illegal copies of our works, in any form, on the Internet, please provide us with the location address or website name immediately so that we can pursue a remedy.

Please contact us at `copyright@packtpub.com` with a link to the suspected pirated material.

We appreciate your help in protecting our authors, and our ability to bring you valuable content.

Questions

You can contact us at `questions@packtpub.com` if you are having a problem with any aspect of the book, and we will do our best to address it.

1
Creating Your BeagleBone Black Development Environment

This book is for secret agents. James Bond is the secret agent who most likely comes to mind, but in today's highly connected world, the real secret agents are to be found in Q branch. Spycraft techniques such as camouflage, listening devices, and palm-print weapons are useful for field agents, but online we need other tools. These tools, like their field agent counterparts, enable you to hide in a crowd, protect secret communication, and prove the identity of other agents. The software and hardware projects in this book use tools relied upon by whistleblowers, journalists protecting their sources, and everyday citizens attempting to access unfiltered information in a strongly censored country.

BeagleBone Black (BBB) is a complete computer that fits inside an Altoid's tin. Its small form factor, low power consumption, and capable performance empower the device to help you secure your privacy and protect your communication online. Before we can build upon these tools, we first need to know how to interact with the BBB. This chapter will introduce you to BBB and suggest a development environment in which you can build the later projects.

In this chapter, you will:

- Learn about BBB and the open source principles behind the project
- Install and use the Emacs editor
- Configure Emacs as your embedded development environment
- Tailor your SSH configuration for usability
- Investigate resources for background information on cryptography, electronics, and Linux

Introducing the BBB

From the BeagleBoard website (`BeagleBoard.org`), which is the nonprofit foundation behind BeagleBoard-xM, BeagleBone, and BBB, the BBB is *a low-cost, community-supported development platform for developers and hobbyists*. The Rev C, which is the latest revision, has impressive specifications including the TI Sitara AM3358 1GHz ARM Cortex-A8 processor, 512 MB of DDR3 RAM, and 4 GB **Embedded Multi-Media Card (eMMC)** for on-board flash. When you take a look at the board, you'll see two 46-pin expansions headers. If you compare it to other hobbyist boards around the same price point, you'll come to the conclusion that the other boards do not contain nearly as much expansion capability. The BBB supports many more **Input/Output (IO)** options, including three I2C buses, multiple serial ports, 65 **General Purpose IO (GPIO)**, multiple **Pulse Width Modulators (PWM)**, and seven analog inputs with built-in **Analog-to-Digital Converters (ADCs)**. If you don't know what all of these are, that's not a problem, as we'll explain the systems that we use throughout the projects.

The quality of the documentation from `BeagleBoard.org` is outstanding. You should read the BBB **System Reference Manual (SRM)**, the official manual for BBB, which is located at `https://github.com/CircuitCo/BeagleBone-Black/blob/master/BBB_SRM.pdf?raw=true`. This is a complete manual that covers connecting the BBB, power options, and boot sequences. Many of the questions asked on the BeagleBoard mailing list and IRC channel can be quickly answered in this manual. The author of this book assumes that you've at least skimmed sections 3, 4, and 5 of the SRM, which means you are aware of the basic capabilities of BBB and are familiar with the physical connectors. There is simply no better reference for the BBB than this document.

Appreciating BBB's commitment to open source hardware

BBB has another very important quality: it is **Open Source Hardware (OSHW)**. OSHW is a relatively new concept, the exact definition of which may confuse people. However, there is a group, the **OSHW Association (OSHWA)**, whose mission is to educate and promote OSHW. Their definition is maintained on their website: `http://www.oshwa.org/definition/`. As with most organizations, a consensus for a definition can be difficult to obtain. The definition of OSHW is well over a page. The complication with defining OSHW from open source software is that hardware is a *physical thing*. There are design files to manufacture hardware, but there are physical components also. To make a software analogy, the compiler for the hardware is the manufacturer. Therefore, the definition of OSHW is carefully constructed and it generally applies to the design files of the hardware.

Alicia Gibb, the Executive Director of OSHWA, gave a TEDx talk called *The Death of Patents and What Comes After* (`https://www.youtube.com/watch?v=z__Sbw1Ax4o`). The talk illustrates how hardware design straddles both copyrights and patent law. Alicia also provides some interesting insights on the incentives behind patents and OSHW.

BBB is OSHW, in that it releases documentation, schematics, **Computer-Aided Design (CAD)** files, **Bill Of Materials (BOM)**, and production files (Gerbers), all under a Creative Commons license. This means that you can not only study the complete design but you are also free to make your own derivative BBB.

Unboxing the BBB and providing power

Unlike Raspberry Pi, BBB is ready out of the box. A recent BBB will come with the Debian distribution of GNU/Linux, henceforth referred to as Debian, installed on the eMMC. eMMC is the on-board flash memory for the BBB. As soon as power is applied to the board, BBB will start to boot from the eMMC. As shown in section three of the SRM, you can connect the BBB directly to your PC with the supplied USB cable. The BBB can also be powered from a 5V barrel jack, where you'll want a wall adapter that can supply up to 1A. If you plan on connecting a mini **liquid-crystal display (LCD)** to the BBB, you may want to use a 2A adapter. You can typically find the output voltage and amperage specifications written on the adapter. You can tell whether the board is powered and running if the blue user **light-emitting diodes (LEDs)** are flashing. Specifically, the LED USER0 will flash in a heartbeat pattern.

Each user LED has a default meaning that corresponds to a specific BBB activity. To further motivate you to read the SRM, the meanings are defined in section 3.4.3 under step 6, *Booting the Board*.

Be very careful when choosing your power supply. The BBB needs 5VDC +/-.25V. Connecting a higher voltage power supply will damage the board.

The BBB can support multiple peripherals such as a keyboard, mouse, and monitor. However, in this book, we'll be using the BBB in a *headless* configuration, which means *without* the monitor. Section 3 of the SRM details the various connection scenarios.

Creating an embedded development environment with Emacs

With the BBB powered, we need to find a way to interact with it. We need a set of tools that will connect to the BBB, send shell commands, and transfer files. This set of tools are your **development environment**. Development environments are a personal choice and there is no shortage of choices. Finding a suitable environment is well worth the time since it will be the main tool, or tools, with which you interface. Your environment needs to be technically capable of performing the tasks you need, but it also needs to be configurable and extensible. The environment that is described here is fully contained within the Emacs editor.

 If you would rather use a specific **Integrated Development Environment** (IDE) such as Eclipse, you can take a look at some useful tutorials at http://derekmolloy.ie/beaglebone/setting-up-eclipse-on-the-beaglebone-for-c-development/ and http://janaxelson.com/eclipse1.htm.

Understanding the complications of embedded development

The history of Emacs is about as long as the history of modern computing. As an editor, Emacs is often overlooked because of its reputation of being outdated and difficult to learn. Emacs can be overwhelming since the interface is different from most modern interfaces. Also, the keybindings were created prior to the invention of modern **Graphical User Interfaces** (GUIs), so the keybindings don't correspond to the shortcuts that you are typically accustomed to. However, there is active development on various Emacs *starter packs*, which provide a smoother Emacs experience. If you keep in mind that Emacs predates your operating system, you may find it easier to accept the Emacs way.

 Many early notable programmers have worked on Emacs, including Guy Steele, Richard Stallman, James Gosling, and Jamie Zawinski. The design of Emacs was presented by Richard Stallman in 1981 to the ACM Conference on Text Processing; the full text is available at https://www.gnu.org/software/emacs/emacs-paper.html.

Embedded development is slightly more complicated than web or desktop development because there are typically two machines involved: the host (your main computer) and the target (your embedded platform). Embedded systems range in capabilities and some run without an operating system, which certainly can't support running a compiler. In this case, the user cross-compiles the code on the host for the target. This can be performed for the BBB, but compiling small programs natively on the BBB does not take too long.

A common recommendation for development on the BBB is to connect to the device over **Secure Shell** (**SSH**) and to use command-line tools. This can be an effective technique, but this limits you to the command line and your terminal emulator. These tools are very powerful and in this context, limited does not mean limited in functionality but limited in the interface.

The one helpful feature of Emacs for embedded development is **Transparent Remote Access Multiple Protocol** or the **TRAMP** mode. In short, the TRAMP mode lets you run Emacs on your host machine, which is most likely more powerful than the BBB, but access files and run commands on the BBB as if they were local. This is transparent in TRAMP; working in this environment feels like you are working on a host, not on an embedded platform. The following screenshot shows the TRAMP feature of Emacs:

This screenshot was captured with Emacs running on Mac OS X, but connected to a BBB with the hostname `slartibartfast`. Everything on this screen is running on the BBB. In the top-left corner, the frame shows a live debugging session with the **GNU debugger** (**GDB**) on a simple C program. In the bottom-left corner, the frame shows the compilation result obtained from running `gcc` on the BBB. In the top-right corner, the frame shows the interactive `gdb` session. Lastly, in the bottom-right corner, the frames show the current directory and a shell, respectively. In the following sections, we'll provide details on how to install Emacs and set up this development environment.

To name your BBB, you'll have to change two files. The first file is `/etc/hostname` and then you'll have to make the same change in `/etc/hosts`. If you struggle to choose a proper name, you will find some comfort in the following XKCD comic:

`https://xkcd.com/910/`

Installing Emacs 24

We'll need Emacs 24.x to take advantage of the **prelude** starter pack by Bozhidar Batsov. Prelude is under active maintenance by Batsov and dedicated prelude users. The code is maintained on GitHub (`https://github.com/bbatsov/prelude`), where there is a detailed README. This software is optional; however, it adds many convenient features and reasonable default configuration settings. Installation procedures for Emacs vary greatly by operating system, but you can consult the following table for the software locations:

OS	Link
Windows	`http://ftp.gnu.org/gnu/emacs/windows/`
Mac OS X	`http://emacsformacosx.com/builds`
Source	`http://ftp.gnu.org/gnu/emacs/emacs-24.3.tar.gz`

If you are a Windows user and are having trouble installing Emacs, consult the guide at `https://www.gnu.org/software/emacs/manual/html_mono/efaq-w32.html`. Mac users should find the binaries listed in the previous section sufficient. If you are using a *nix machine, you can either use your package manager to install Emacs or build from the source. If you use the package manager, be sure to install Emacs' major version 24. In a Debian-based system, the command is `apt-get install emacs24`.

Installing the prelude

The Emacs prelude software can be installed by typing the following command:

```
curl -L http://git.io/epre | sh
```

Downloading the example code

You can download the example code files for all Packt books you have purchased from your account at http://www.packtpub.com. If you purchased this book elsewhere, you can visit http://www.packtpub.com/support and register to have the files e-mailed directly to you.

If you are wary of shortened URLs, take a look at the prelude README for alternate installation instructions, which is available at https://github.com/bbatsov/prelude. The installer will complain about any missing packages that you need to install. Once complete, you should run Emacs. If you have installed a binary version for your OS, double-clicking on the icon should suffice. On a command line, just type emacs to launch the program. On the initial start, Emacs will attempt to go to the Emacs package managers and download additional software. It will then byte-compile the source files, so it takes a minute or two. Once this is complete, close Emacs and open it again; you should see something similar to what is shown in the following screen:

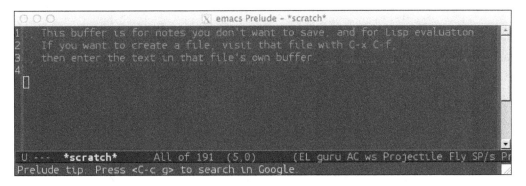

Yes, Emacs has its own package manager and Emacs-specific repositories that provide the Emacs Lisp Package. See the following blog post by Batsov for a deeper look at Emacs packaging:

http://batsov.com/articles/2012/02/19/package-management-in-emacs-the-good-the-bad-and-the-ugly/

Learning how to learn about Emacs

Emacs has too many features. Here's a tongue-in-cheek joke: *Emacs is an operating system that is in need of a good editor*. This section will illustrate the basic skills that one needs to use Emacs and more importantly, to learn how to use Emacs. One of the best features of Emacs is the immense built-in help. If you have never run Emacs before, press *Ctrl-h t*, abbreviated *C-h t*. This means that while holding the *Ctrl* key, press *h*, then release it, and then press *t*. Also, note that the Emacs commands are case sensitive. *C-H T* means to press *Ctrl + Shift + H*, then hit *Shift + T*, whereas *C-h t* is performed without the shift modifier. You'll be presented with the interactive Emacs tutorial. This tutorial will teach you the fundamentals of Emacs. In the tutorial, you'll see references to a meta key, which you will be hard pressed to find on your keyboard. Command sequences, such as *M-x*, mean to hold down the meta key while pressing *x*. Depending on your system, the meta key may be *Alt* or *Option*. If neither of these work, you can press the *Esc* key and release it to provide meta.

The tutorial is very good and for the rest of this chapter, it is assumed that you have completed this tutorial or have an equivalent level of knowledge to understand the more advanced features.

Some other helpful resources to learn Emacs are Sacha Chua's *How to Learn Emacs* diagram (http://sachachua.com/blog/wp-content/uploads/2013/05/How-to-Learn-Emacs-v2-Large.png) and the official *Emacs 24 Reference Card* (https://www.gnu.org/software/emacs/refcards/pdf/refcard.pdf).

If you are a vi user, there is a mode that emulates most vi keybindings, called the viper mode (http://www.emacswiki.org/emacs/ViperMode).

Streamlining the SSH connections

Even if you don't use Emacs, you'll find yourself frequently connecting to the BBB with SSH. If you run the BBB from the USB cable attached to your PC, then the default Internet Protocol (IP) address of the BBB will be 192.168.7.2. However, if you want to download software directly to the BBB, as you will need to do in order to complete these projects, you'll have to forward your Internet connection from the PC to the BBB. Also, when powered from the USB directly, there is typically a 500mA current limit. When the BBB is powering expansion boards or other peripherals, it'll need to be powered from a 5V DC plug that can supply up to 1A. As a result of these two issues, you may find it much more convenient to run the BBB from a 5V power supply and connect the Ethernet cable into your home network directly.

When you do this, the IP address will most likely be assigned by your router and will only be known to your router. This will leaving you staring at the BBB pontificating over its IP address.

Discovering the IP address of your networked BBB

There are a few ways to discover the IP address of your device. The first way is to log in to your router and look up the IP address. This is a quick method but as there are numerous routers, you'll have to consult your router's documentation on how to accomplish this.

You can also use the nmap utility to conduct a quick **ping scan** on your network. Assuming that you are familiar with the IP address of your own network, you should be able to see a new device. If you are running an apt-based distribution, you can install nmap with sudo apt-get install nmap. If you are on a Mac, you can use the homebrew package manager (http://brew.sh/) and install it with brew install nmap. Windows users should download the binary from http://nmap. org/download.html#windows. Once it is installed, you'll want to run a command similar to the following:

```
nmap -sn 192.168.1.0/24
```

Replace 192.168.1.0 with the appropriate address for your network. /24 is the **Classless Inter-Domain Routing (CIDR)** notation for the subnet mask. In this case, /24 means use a subnet mask of 24 bits of 1's, or 255.255.255.0. The -sn option directs nmap to conduct a ping scan.

If you are still unable to determine the IP address, you can buy a USB-to-serial adapter cable. BBB has a serial debug header located inboard of the P9 header. You can attach the USB-to-serial adapter to BBB's serial debug header, as shown in the following image:

In this figure, pin 1 (which is the black wire) is the ground, pin 4 is receive, and pin 5 is transmit. Once physically attached, you'll need a terminal emulator to connect over the serial connection. GNU Screen is a widely available, free, and robust software that will connect with the following command; just replace /dev/tty.XXXX with the file of your connection:

```
screen /dev/tty.PL2303-004014FA 115200
```

Lastly, you can set a static IP for your BBB. Your router may support a static lease feature, which will assign the IP of your choosing to the device when it performs a **Dynamic Host Configuration Protocol (DHCP)** request. The lease on this request can be indefinite and, therefore, effectively provides a *static* IP. You can also set the IP statically on your device, but then you will have to manage conflicts manually. Therefore, the preferred method is to let the router handle this situation.

 To find a serial debugging cable, see the eLinux page at http://elinux.org/Beagleboard:BeagleBone_Black_Serial.

To take full advantage of the SSH configuration options in the following section, you'll want to have a static IP set. Otherwise, you will have to repeat the previous steps to determine the IP address of the device when your router power cycles or if the BBB is disconnected for a few days.

> If you prefer to use a WiFi connection instead of Ethernet, be aware that there are issues with some dongles. Refer to this eLinux page for supported adapters: `http://elinux.org/Beagleboard:BeagleBon eBlack#WIFI_Adapters`.

Editing the SSH configuration file

In order to connect to BBB, you need to type something similar to the following, but use the BBB's IP address from the previous section:

`ssh debian@192.168.1.10`

> If you are a Windows user, you should consider using more Unixy tools on your host since the BBB is running Debian anyway. You can install Cygwin (`https://www.cygwin.com/`), which will give you a nice shell with the associated command-line tools. Or, consider downloading VirtualBox (`https://www.virtualbox.org/`) and installing a GNU/ Linux distribution in a virtual machine.

The default username is `debian` and the default password is `temppwd`. If you only have one device, typing this command may be manageable. Once you start collecting BBBs, Raspberry Pis, pcDuinos, Cubieboards, Arduinos with a WiFly Shield, and so on, you will have to remember each IP, username, and password. This can become annoying. Fortunately, there are a few tricks that you can use to improve this situation.

First, you'll need a SSH private key. If you don't already have a key, you can generate one on your host with the following command:

`ssh-keygen -t rsa -b 4096`

Now edit the `~/.ssh/config` file. If you are doing this in Emacs, you can press *C-x C-f* and then type `~/.ssh/config`. Emacs keybindings are all bound to Emacs Lisp commands (technically, there are a few basic commands implemented in C). The keybinding *C-x C-f* is bound to the `find-file` function. An alternate, albeit longer, way to open a file is to press *M-x*, type `find-file`, then open the file of your choice.

Add the following section to your ~/.ssh/config file, replacing HostName with the IP address of your BBB:

```
Host bbb
     HostName 192.168.1.10
     User debian
```

Now, you can SSH into the BBB just by typing ssh bbb. Add as many servers as you want here and give them descriptive names, and this will you manage your connections.

Configuring password-less login

If you've followed the above step, then connecting to your BBB is now simplified with the exception of entering the password. Connect to your BBB and run the ssh-keygen command on BBB. This will create the .ssh directory for you. You don't have to generate an SSH key; you could just create the .ssh directory, but chances are that you may need an SSH key anyway and this will accomplish both tasks.

Before you log out, we need to perform one bit of maintenance. We need to regenerate the SSH host key, the key on the BBB, since the key on your device was cloned from an image. The process involves just a few commands but requires running them as root. You can either type sudo su and become root and run the commands, or append sudo in front of each command in the following code snippet, based off the Nix Craft article at http://www.cyberciti.biz/faq/howto-regenerate-openssh-host-keys/:

```
rm /etc/ssh/ssh_host_*
dpkg-reconfigure openssh-server
```

This will delete your existing SSH host key and regenerate it from scratch. Since the host key has changed, we need to update your SSH client on you main computer. If you log in to the BBB again, you will probably receive a warning that the fingerprint doesn't match because you changed it. You can remove the old entry from your client by typing the following (you may have to use the IP address instead of bbb):

```
ssh-keygen -R bbb
```

Alternatively, you can edit ~/.ssh/known_hosts directly and remove the entry.

With the new SSH key on the BBB and the old entry in known_hosts removed, log back in to the BBB just to make sure everything is working. Log back out and return to the terminal on your host. After executing the following command, you will no longer be prompted for a password:

```
cat .ssh/id_rsa.pub | ssh bbb 'cat >> .ssh/authorized_keys'
```

This will copy your public SSH key to the BBB, which will be recognized in the SSH handshake as an authorized key, and therefore, it will not require you to enter the `debian` user's password.

Most likely, you will need to perform this operation again and you may not want to refer to this book to find this command. You can add this function to your `.bashrc` file or an equivalent for further ease of use:

```
ssh_upload(){
  if [[ $# -ne 1 ]]; then
    echo "usage: host\nNOTE: host should be set in ~/.ssh/config"
    else
    cat ~/.ssh/id_rsa.pub | ssh $1 'cat >> ~/.ssh/authorized_keys'
    fi
}
```

Then, you can add your key to servers with:

ssh_upload bbb

Don't forget to reload your `.bashrc` file to gain this function with:

```
source ~/.bashrc
```

Logging out and in again will also work.

Running an SSH agent to control access to your SSH keys

Now you don't have to enter the `debian` account password each time you log in to the BBB, but now you do have to enter the password for your SSH private key. This is equally annoying. However, we can fix this by running `ssh-agent`. Installing and configuring `ssh-agent` is OS-dependent, and instructions are easy to find online. Once `ssh-agent` is running, you'll typically have to enter your SSH private key password when you log in and if you make an SSH connection within a certain time period, you'll instantly connect to the remote server without any additional password entry.

Connecting to BBB with TRAMP

Now that we've configured SSH, we will now have an easier time connecting to BBB with TRAMP and Emacs. Emacs has a built-in directory editor called `dired`, which can be invoked by pressing *C-x d*. We want to open `dired` on the BBB to view the remote files. Press *C-x d* and then enter the following for the directory: `/ssh:bbb:/home/debian`. A screen similar to the following should immediately open, which will show you the contents of the home directory:

```
Emacs Prelude – debian — (74 x 23)
1   /ssh:slartibartfast:/home/debian:
2   total 140
3   drwxr-xr-x 8 debian debian  4096 Aug  1 16:24 .
4   drwxr-xr-x 3 root   root    4096 Jul  6 23:23 ..
5   -rw-------  1 debian debian  2440 Jul 31 18:27 .bash_history
6   -rw-r--r--  1 debian debian   220 Apr 19 04:38 .bash_logout
7   -rw-r--r--  1 debian debian  3392 Apr 19 04:38 .bashrc
8   drwx------  3 debian debian  4096 Jul 12 16:12 .emacs.d
9   drwx------  2 debian debian  4096 Jul 11 15:19 .gnupg
10  -rw-r--r--  1 debian debian   675 Apr 19 04:38 .profile
11  drwx------  2 debian debian  4096 Jul 30 17:37 .ssh
12  -rw-------  1 debian debian     3 Aug  1 16:24 .tramp_history
13  drwxr-xr-x 2 debian debian  4096 Jul  6 23:23 bin
14  -rw-r--r--  1 debian debian 81298 Jul 31 23:36 emacs_dired.jpg
15  drwxr-xr-x 7 debian debian  4096 Jul 12 15:21 repos
16  drwxr-xr-x 2 debian debian  4096 Aug  1 00:04 test
17  -rw-r--r--  1 debian debian    14 Jul 31 18:10 test.py
18  -rw-r--r--  1 debian debian    22 Jul 31 23:49 test.txt

-:%%@  debian          All of 949  (5,48)     (Dired by name company Proj
```

All the basic Emacs navigation commands work in `dired`, so you can navigate the directory and press enter to open a file or another directory. The ^ key will navigate you to the parent directory. You can also click on the directories or files to open them.

> If the `tramp-default-method` variable is set to `ssh`, then you can shorten your URLs to `/bbb:/home/debian`. You can view the state of the variable by evaluating it. To evaluate Emacs Lisp, press *M-:* and then type `tramp-default-method` and the mini buffer should reply with `ssh`.

For more information on `dired` or anything about Emacs, you can view the built-in documentation by pressing *C-h r*. If you scroll or search (by pressing *C-s*), you'll find the `dired` manual on that page. The manual uses the info viewer, and you can read about this by pressing *C-h i* to get the main information page and then pressing *h*.

One of the features of Emacs is its extensibility. Presumably, you will be connecting to the BBB often, pressing *C-x d*, and typing /ssh:bbb:/home/debian can be tiresome. Let's define a new key sequence to make this easier. Switch to the scratch buffer in Emacs. This can be done by pressing *C-x b*, then typing *scratch, and then hitting *Tab + Enter*. Paste the following code:

```
(global-set-key
 [(control x) (control y)]
 (lambda ()
   "Open a dired buffer on the BBB"
   (interactive)
   (dired "/ssh:bbb:/home/debian")))
```

Position the point, what Emacs calls the cursor, after the last parenthesis. Then, press *C-x C-e* to evaluate this snippet of Emacs Lisp. The mini buffer should echo the result. Now press *C-x C-y* and you should see the home directory of BBB. Congratulations! You've just customized Emacs! If you restart Emacs, however, you'll lose this convenient function, so you need to save it. If you are using the Emacs prelude, customizations should go in ~/.emacs.d/personal/foo.el. You can save this buffer with *C-x C-s* and specify the filename.

If you enjoy using Emacs, you will probably enjoy changing Emacs, which can be done with Emacs Lisp. Of course, Emacs contains a great manual to learn Emacs Lisp, *An Introduction to Programming in Emacs Lisp*. It can be accessed by pressing *C-h i d* and then you can either scroll down to the manual or press m, type Emacs Lisp, and then press *Tab* for tabcompletion to *Emacs Lisp Intro*.

Running commands from Emacs

If you are currently looking at the dired buffer in Emacs, then Emacs is aware that you are on a remote machine. Certain commands are TRAMP-aware and will execute remotely. For example, *M-!* will execute a shell command. When used over TRAMP, it will execute the shell command remotely. Try using *M-!* with touch test.txt. Now press *g* to refresh dired. You should now see test.txt. If you edit this file by navigating to it in dired and then pressing *Enter*, you will now be editing the file remotely. Technically, you are editing a local copy of this buffer but when you save it with *C-x C-s*, it will send the changes over to the BBB.

There is a benefit to this system. If the SSH connection drops, for whatever reason, the buffer is still in RAM on your local machine. Once the connection is restored, Emacs will save the buffer. Emacs acts as a session manager for your remote connections and will transparently reconnect when needed.

If you open a C file in Emacs, Emacs will apply C-aware syntax highlighting, but it can also compile and debug over TRAMP. To compile, invoke *M-x*, type `compile`, and supply the compile command. If there is a makefile, then `make` should suffice; otherwise, provide the full `gcc` compilation string. The benefit of using the compile function is that Emacs will be aware of compilation errors and you can jump to each one with *C-x`*. Lastly, if you install `gdb` on BBB, you debug with `gdb` from your host computer. Assuming that you compiled your program with debug symbols, if you are looking at the source file in the current buffer, you can press *M-x*, and then type `gdb`.

You'll have to provide the `gdb` command, which is something such as `gdb nameofexec -i=mi`. Emacs will remotely launch `gdb` and open an interactive session. If you set breakpoints, Emacs will switch over to the code buffer and show you where the instruction pointer has stopped in the code.

Lastly, you can run a shell inside Emacs on the remote system as well. If you are in a TRAMP-aware buffer, pressing *M-x* and then typing `shell` will open a remote shell. You can perform all your development actions while never leaving Emacs. Emacs can also act as your mail reader, calculator, IRC client, and even play Tetris (by pressing *M-x*, and then typing `Tetris`). Emacs is a cross platform editor, so if you learn how to use Emacs once, you can use it as your development environment on any machine.

 XKCD fans of comic 378, should press *M-x* and then type `butterfly`. Be sure to respond `yes` to the question *Do you really want to unleash the powers of the butterfly?* For background on *M-x* butterfly, see `https://xkcd.com/378/`

Using Emacs dired to copy files to and from BBB

Another routine and tedious task is to copy files from the host to the target or vice versa. Most likely, you can use the command line and a tool such as `scp` to send files back and forth. Emacs `dired` using TRAMP will make this task much simpler. In a `dired` buffer, press *C* to invoke the `dired-do-copy` function. This will prompt you for the destination. If you specify a remote address such as `/ssh:bbb:/home/debian`, then `dired` will copy the files over SSH. You can copy multiple files by marking them with *m* and then pressing *C*. The reverse, copying files from BBB to the host, is the same process. This prevents you from having to drop to a shell and use `scp`.

There are many resources online to learn Emacs. If you are an IRC user, the `#emacs` channel on `Freenode` is the watering hole of many experienced Emacs users. The Emacs wiki is also a good starting point for Emacs research, which has a Emacs newbie entry (`http://www.emacswiki.org/emacs/EmacsNewbie`). The built-in help system is quite extensive. To receive help on the help system, press *C-h ?*.

Finding additional background information

The projects in the book are, for the most part, self-contained. However, they do assume that you have some background knowledge in working with a GNU/Linux system, electronics, and some cryptographic concepts. The following sections list some resources in each area for those who want to seek further information.

Finding additional cryptography resources

The projects in this book all use some sort of cryptography. If you are familiar with terms such as asymmetric cryptography, digital signatures, and message authentication codes, then you should be OK. If not, you will still be able to complete the projects but you may not appreciate the theory behind them.

As this is not a book on cryptography, a primer here will not provide enough detail for a beginner and will be woefully inadequate for someone familiar with the material. If cryptography is new to you, you can still proceed with the book. In the beginning of each chapter, there is some tailored background to explain the material, which should be enough for you to understand what the project is trying to accomplish. Once complete, hopefully, you'll be interested in cryptography and you can get more information from the following resources.

For a gentle introduction to the topic, *Cryptography: A Very Short Introduction* by *Fred Piper and Sean Murphy, Oxford University Press, 2002*, is good starting point. However, as the title suggests, it lacks technical depth. *Understanding Cryptography: A Textbook for Students and Practitioners* by *Christof Paar et. al., Springer, 2010*, is a more detailed introduction. For the more inquisitive readers, *Introduction to Modern Cryptography* by *Jonathan Katz and Yehuda Lindell, Chapman and Hall/CRC, 2007*, is a good up-to-date reference.

If lectures better suit you, you are in luck. Khan Academy has some interesting and free mini-lectures covering ancient cryptography up to RSA (`https://www.khanacademy.org/computing/computer-science/cryptography`). Another free resource is Coursera, which has three cryptography classes, *Cryptography I and II* taught by Standford Professor Dan Boneh, and a Cryptography class on modern cryptography taught by Jonathan Katz. The links for these classes are `https://www.coursera.org/course/crypto`, `https://www.coursera.org/course/crypto2`, and `https://www.coursera.org/course/cryptography`, respectively.

Finding additional electronics resources

Similarly, this book assumes some basic electronics knowledge. If you are looking for a book, *Practical Electronics for Inventors, Third Edition* by *Paul Scherz and Simon Monk, Tab Books, 2013*, is a solid and approachable reference. Khan Academy has a series on basic concepts in electricity and magnetism as well (`https://www.khanacademy.org/science/physics/electricity-and-magnetism`). Dave Jones EEVBlog is an entertaining and informative video blog that covers many areas of electronics and should be of interest to hobbyists in electronics (`http://www.eevblog.com/`).

Finding additional Debian resources

For those new to Debian, there is an comprehensive and free handbook available online called *The Debian Administrator's Handbook* by *Raphaël Hertzog and Roland Mas, Freexian SARL, 2014*, at `http://debian-handbook.info/browse/stable/`. At a minimum, you should read *Chapter 6, Maintenance and Updates: The APT Tools*, of this book, which details how to use the apt set of tools for package management. There is also a free class offered by the Linux Foundation and edX called *Introduction to Linux* (`https://www.edx.org/course/linuxfoundationx/linuxfoundationx-lfs101x-introduction-1621`). The class is fairly recent and it does not appear to use the Debian distribution, but it does seem like a representative course on generic Linux information. Lastly, there are several Debian IRC channels on the OFTC IRC network. Most of the channels start with `#debian` and you should be able to ask specific questions there. The BeagleBoard channel is `#beagle` on `Freenode`, and there will be people there who can help answer your questions as well.

Summary

In this chapter, you learned how to connect to your BBB. `BeagleBoard.org` has streamlined the out-of-box experience, so there is a minimal setup on the device itself. You learned that the definitive reference manual for the BBB is the *System Reference Manual*, which should be your first stop for hardware-related questions about BBB. You learned about Emacs and how to create an embedded development environment with Emacs. Lastly, we identified several resources to find additional information on cryptography, electronics, and Linux.

In the rest of this book, you will build projects around the most popular and trusted software security packages: Tor, GNU Privacy Guide, and Off-the-Record messaging, all of which are actively used and maintained. In the next chapter, we'll use Tor and the BBB to help strengthen a censorship-resistant network.

2
Circumventing Censorship with a Tor Bridge

In this chapter, you'll configure your **BeagleBone Black (BBB)** to run a bridge in the Tor network. This bridge will allow you and others to access the Internet more anonymously and provide an anti-censorship gateway. We'll add a simple hardware control interface to BBB so that we can see and adjust the bandwidth usage of the bridge in real time. We'll call this project BeagleBridge.

This chapter will discuss the following topics:

- An introduction to Tor
- The difference between a Tor relay and bridge
- Obfuscated Tor proxies
- How to download and install Tor on BBB
- How to configure BBB as a Tor bridge running an obfuscated proxy
- How to add hardware controls to adjust the bridge from a front panel

Learning about Tor

In this project, you will learn how to use Tor, a tool and network designed to protect your anonymity online. Tor originally developed from research, sponsored by the U.S. Naval Research Laboratory, on **onion routing** (Dingledine, Mathewson, and Syverson, 2004). In onion routing, the client builds a circuit of nodes in an overlay network, which is a network built on top of an existing network. The Tor network is an overlay network that runs on the Internet, although it can run on separate networks. The client sends a message to each node, which is specifically encrypted for that node, asking the node to send it to the next node in the circuit. Each node peels back a layer of encryption and forwards the result to the next hop in the circuit, and hence, the **onion analogy**. The last node contains the client's actual message, which is forwarded to the destination server.

Onion routing provides anonymity because the destination server does not know the IP address of the client. Typically, when you use your browser to access the Internet, the browser creates a **Transmission Control Protocol** (**TCP**) connection that originates from your system and terminates at the website you are trying to visit. The address for TCP is provided by the **Internet Protocol** (**IP**). Each IP datagram contains a source and destination IP address. As datagrams arrive at the server, the server can read the source IP address. This is generally useful as the server needs this address to return your data. However, this also means that the server knows your IP address, which is where you live on the Internet. Your IP address alone reveals information about you, such as the country in which you live and your **Internet Service Provider** (**ISP**). Geolocating by an IP address can be accurate to the zip code level, when you use United States as an example.

> **Tor**, originally an acronym for **The Onion Router**, is now simply referred to as *Tor*, not *TOR*. When you ask questions on the Tor mailing list or IRC channels, Tor developers will appreciate it if you make note of this subtlety.

The following diagram shows this routing. In this case, Alice is a client who connects to the first node of her circuit, which happens to be running on your BBB. This BBB unwraps a layer and forwards Alice's communication to the middle node. The middle node does the same to the final (exit) node. The exit node sends Alice's original message to the destination server named Bob. The green arrows show internal Tor connections that are encrypted. The connection from the exit node to Bob is shown as an unencrypted connection because this traffic is not part of the Tor network. From Bob's perspective, the IP originator of this connection is the exit node. However, the true originator is Alice whose IP is hidden by the Tor network.

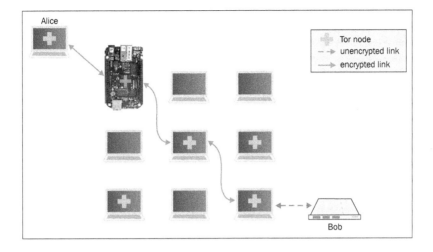

The response to this information by many individuals is:

"So what? Why do I care if the website I'm visiting knows my IP address?"

The website, which knows the data you requested, now knows your location. This information could be combined with other public information, for example, to conduct a **linkage attack**. A linkage attack is an attempt at deanonymization by combining information from multiple sources. For example, let's say you are searching for information on a rare medical condition. You post a question on a forum, under a pseudonym, asking for information. However, the website, and anybody passively monitoring your connection (if it wasn't encrypted), knows your general location as well as your question. Your medical condition is most prevalent in Hispanic females in their seventies. Using your IP address combined with knowledge about your medical condition, one can conduct a linkage attack possibly using public census data to reveal your identity.

Tor protects against this kind of attacks by encrypting your traffic through the Tor network and masking your IP address. To the remote website, your IP address will be that of the last node in the Tor network, known as an exit relay.

Appreciating the various users of Tor

A wide range of people use Tor for daily Internet access. Individuals who don't want their ISP to collect information on the websites they visit, perhaps because they are seeking information on sensitive topics, use Tor. Government agents and the military use Tor. After all, it's difficult to go undercover online if the IP address you are connecting FROM resolves to `fbi.gov`. Tor is used by whistleblowers, such as Edward Snowden, to disclose information to the press. It is also used by normal citizens when a government blocks access to the Internet. In late March 2014, when the Turkish government attempted to ban access to Twitter, the number of Tor users in Turkey jumped from around 25,000 to just under 70,000 in about two weeks.

Tor publishes, via a wide range of interactive graphs, numerous metrics on who is using Tor and where they're using it from. The users spike in Turkey can be seen in the graph available at `https://metrics.torproject.org/users.html?graph=userstats-relay-country&start=2014-01-04&end=2014-04-04&country=tr&events=off#userstats-relay-country`.

Understanding Tor relays

Tor relays are the individual nodes in the Tor network. A node is some type of computer that is running the Tor software. These relays route messages throughout the network. Exit nodes, which are the last nodes in the circuit, send the clients' messages to the destination service. One of the interesting aspects of Tor is that most of the nodes are run by volunteers. These relay operators volunteer their bandwidth, time, and energy bill to increase the capacity of the Tor network. The Tor Project encourages individuals to run relays in order to add to the diversity of the network. The motivation behind this recommendation is that it is easier to hide in a crowd—it's difficult to hide in a crowd of one person.

Understanding Tor bridges

In 2006, in response to an increased Internet censorship, the Tor project added an anticensorship feature called a bridge relay or simply, a bridge (Dingledine, 2006). A bridge is a special form of a relay—it's not listed in the public relay directory. Strong Internet censors were able to block access to Tor through several methods. One method that was effective was to look up all the public relays, which were only a thousand or so at the time, and deny access to those IP addresses. Therefore, bridge relays were created and distributed by less public means in order to allow users to access the Tor network. If a client could access the bridge, which was already connected to Tor, then the client could access the Internet. In this context, less public means a distribution mechanism that does not work via the public relay list.

Using obfuscated proxies and pluggable transports

Censors were still able to block access to Tor; the technique was to identify the traffic patterns generated by Tor and block the connection. In 2010, Jacob Appelbaum and Nick Mathewson of the Tor Project suggested a method to obfuscate the Tor traffic between the client and the bridge in order to thwart deep packet inspection. As the obfuscation mechanism might need to change, and has changed in fact, the Tor Project wanted a generic protocol to allow different obfuscated proxies to run. This abstraction was known as **pluggable transport**.

In this chapter, we will set up your BBB to run as a Tor bridge, running an obfuscated proxy, using the obfs3 pluggable transport.

Realizing the limitations of Tor

Tor is one of the best tools currently available to protect anonymity. However, like all the security tools discussed in this book, there are limits to its protection. First of all, Tor's threat model does not hold up to a global passive adversary. Such an adversary can passively monitor the entire Internet. If an adversary can monitor the entire Internet, then it can correlate the traffic entering the Tor network with the traffic leaving the network and can possibly deanonymize Tor clients. One of the trade-offs of this design is that Tor is a low-latency system, meaning that you can access the Internet using normal protocols such as HTTP without experiencing much delay. This is one of the reasons why diversity in the Tor network is important. If all the relays were in a particular country, it might be easier for that country to monitor the traffic. However, currently it is thought to be difficult, in spite of the recent leaks provided by Edward Snowden, for such an adversary to monitor the entire Internet.

> Roger Dingledine of the Tor Project commented on NSA's exploits of Tor with the following:
>
> *"The good news is that they [the NSA] went for a browser exploit, meaning there's no indication that they can break the Tor protocol or do traffic analysis on the Tor network. Infecting the laptop, phone, or desktop is still the easiest way to learn about the human behind the keyboard."*
>
> The full text and additional commentary is available on the Tor website (`https://blog.torproject.org/blog/yes-we-know-about-guardian-article`).

Also, Tor will not automatically encrypt all your traffic. If you request information over unencrypted HTTP, the Tor exit node you use will relay this unencrypted information to its destination. A malicious exit node can monitor or manipulate your traffic; therefore, it's always best to use encrypted sessions, such as HTTPS, over Tor. Tor does not protect all your traffic just because you are running Tor. Applications generally need to be configured to use Tor. Even if you set up a transparent proxy on your home network and route all of your traffic through that proxy, the malware or exploits in your browser may leak your identity. This is why the Tor Project recommends that you use the Tor Browser, which essentially is a forked version of Mozilla Firefox that has been patched especially to not leak your identity. Lastly, Tor can't protect your identity if you choose to reveal it. If you decide to log in to Facebook over Tor, you've just told Facebook who you are and that you are using Tor since all the Tor exit nodes are public.

 An easy way to use Tor more securely is to use it only from Tails (`https://tails.boum.org/`), which is a custom Linux distribution that will boot from various media. Tails is a collection of free software and includes numerous correctly configured tools to help protect your confidentiality and anonymity.

The impact and benefits of running a Tor bridge

So, why run a Tor bridge on BBB? The impact and benefits of Tor is in the network. The more the Tor servers, the more the resources in the network. Many users in developed nations have high-speed Internet connections that are orders of magnitude faster than in countries where access to censor-free Internet is restricted. A bridge is likely to receive less traffic than a relay, as there are fewer bridge users than normal Tor users. Most likely, the limiting performance factor for your bridge will be your home network's upload speed. This can be a constraining factor if you are running a relay, but as a bridge, you are most likely helping those in precarious Internet situations and any donated bandwidth is appreciated. Lastly, running a bridge on BBB has the extra advantage of a low impact on your electric bill, as BBB will only draw about 460mA when loading a web page according to the BeagleBone Black System Reference Manual.

Installing Tor on BBB

The instructions provided in the following sections are geared towards the user running BeagleBridge on a home network. The bridge will consume some otherwise unused bandwidth and donate it to the Tor network. You should check your ISP's Terms of Service before running a server to see whether it's permitted. Also, you'll need to configure port forwarding from your home router. As there are numerous devices, each with their own configuration mechanism, you should consult your router's manual on how to enable port forwarding.

Installing Tor from the development repository

The Tor images in the official Debian repository are not as up to date as those from the Tor Project. We'll use the Tor Project's development repository to retrieve the latest software. This is especially important when you are running a bridge, as the bridge and the pluggable transport software are updated frequently.

 The latest instructions as well as the latest GPG fingerprint can be found on the Tor Project's website (https://www.torproject.org/docs/debian). The following steps explain the installation procedure, but you should cross-reference them with the published instructions.

Edit /etc/apt/sources.list by adding the following lines:

```
deb http://deb.torproject.org/torproject.org wheezy main
deb http://deb.torproject.org/torproject.org tor-experimental-0.2.5.x-wheezy main
```

Next, add the GPG key used to sign these Tor packages:

```
gpg --keyserver keys.gnupg.net --recv 886DDD89
gpg --export A3C4F0F979CAA22CDBA8F512EE8CBC9E886DDD89 | sudo apt-key add -
```

Then, issue the following command:

```
sudo apt-get update
```

The Tor Project recommends that you add the GPG key ring with the following command:

```
sudo apt-get install deb.torproject.org-keyring
```

Tor needs an up-to-date time as it enforces the time validity on certificates. In a later chapter, we'll show you how to keep time with a dedicated **Real Time Clock (RTC)**. For now, update your clock from the **Network Time Protocol (NTP)** as follows:

```
sudo ntpdate -b -u pool.ntp.org
```

Install Tor:

```
sudo apt-get install tor
```

Then, install `obfsproxy`. Obfsproxy is the software that implements the obfuscated proxy and allows various pluggable transports. Obfsproxy uses Python Twisted library, an event-driven networking engine, which will install around 17 MB of packages in total:

```
sudo apt-get install obfsproxy
```

While we are installing software, let's install the Stem Python package. Stem is a Python controller library for Tor, and we'll be using it later to interact with our bridge. The easiest method is to install it with `pip`:

```
sudo pip install stem
```

Configuring Tor for BBB

Under Debian, the configuration file for Tor is `/etc/tor/torrc`. Before editing `/etc/tor/torrc`, you should first take a backup. This `torrc` file is available for download at `https://github.com/jbdatko/beagle-bone-for-secret-agents/blob/master/ch2/torrc`. We will discuss more interesting aspects of this configuration file in the following sections. When you are ready, replace `/etc/tor/torrc` with the following:

```
# We are running a relay, no need for the SocksPort
SocksPort 0
# Extra logging is nice
Log notice file /var/log/tor/notices.log
# Run in the background
RunAsDaemon 1
# The following two lines are so we can connect with the
## Tor Stem library over the control port
ControlPort 9051
CookieAuthentication 1
# The is the Onion Router (OR) Port for normal relay operation
ORPort 9001
# Your bridge's nickname, change!
Nickname changeme
```

```
# Bandwidth settings
RelayBandwidthRate 520 KB # Throttle traffic to 520 KB/s
RelayBandwidthBurst 640 KB # But allow burts up to 640 KB/s
# You put a real email here, but consider making a new account
## or alias address
ContactInfo Random Person <nobody AT example dot com>
# Do not exit traffic
ExitPolicy reject *:* # no exits allowed
# Yes, we want to be a bridge
BridgeRelay 1
# Use the obfs3 pluggable transport
ServerTransportPlugin obfs3 exec /usr/bin/obfsproxy managed
# Enable extra bridge statistics collection
ExtORPort auto
# A nice option for embedded platforms to minimize writes
# to eMMC or SD card
AvoidDiskWrites 1
```

Adding contact details to the torrc file

At minimum, you should change the `Nickname` field and `ContactInfo`. The `Nickname` field is a shorter way to refer to your bridge; however, your bridge's fingerprint is always the best method as it is unique. The `ContactInfo` field allows the Tor project to send you an e-mail if there is a problem with your bridge. You can create an e-mail alias if you are concerned about receiving spam. Just be sure to monitor this account for infrequent e-mails from the Tor project.

Tuning the bandwidth usage of your bridge

Tor's man page will describe most of these settings in detail, but some warrant extra explanation. The bandwidth settings, `RelayBandwidthRate` and `RelayBandwidthBurst`, are tunable bandwidth settings, and in a later section, we will connect our hardware controls to manipulate these settings. The rate and the burst are in kilobytes per second, not in the more common kilo or *megabits* per second, so watch your units.

Understanding Tor exit policies

A bridge, by definition, is the entry point to the Tor network. As such, the exit policy, which will allow traffic to exit the Tor network from the server, should be the following:

ExitPolicy reject *:*

This prevents your server from running as an exit node. If you do decide to run an exit node, be prepared to receive some complaints from your ISP if you are running it on a home network. This is why the Tor Project and the Electronic Frontier Foundation recommend that you *don't* run an exit relay on a home network. A thorough, legal FAQ prepared by the Electronic Frontier Foundation can be found at `https://www.torproject.org/eff/tor-legal-faq.html.en`.

Setting bridge-specific settings

There are three bridge specific settings: `BridgeRelay`, `ServerTransportPlugin`, and `ExtORPort`. The `BridgeRelay` setting is the key setting that defines your relay as a bridge. Your bridge's meta information is published in the bridge database instead of the public directory server, which keeps your bridge's IP less public than a Tor relay's IP address. `ServerTransportPlugin` defines which pluggable transport proxy your bridge supports. Currently, ScrambleSuit is the latest promising pluggable transport technology. However, obfs3, which is the transport enabled in our bridge configuration example, is slightly more mature and it is the more conservative recommendation. Lastly, `ExtORPort` allows the gathering and reporting of bridge statistics to the Tor Project.

> For those who are interested in running the ScrambleSuit obfsproxy, take a look at the following link on how to configure your bridge: `https://lists.torproject.org/pipermail/tor-relays/2014-February/003886.html`.

Starting your new Tor bridge

With the time updated and the configuration set, it's time to turn on the bridge. At the moment, the bridge should be able to make a connection to the Tor network, but it will not be able to accept incoming connections as we have not yet configured port forwarding from your router. However, the obfsproxy port is randomly assigned, so we need to run the bridge first to find the port. Restart the Tor service with the following command:

```
sudo service tor restart
```

Next, let's check the log to see whether Tor has started correctly:

```
tail -n 20 /var/log/tor/notices.log
```

If you see something like the following, then your Tor client's behavior is working:

```
Mar 25 21:37:43.000 [notice] Tor has successfully opened a circuit. Looks
like client functionality is working.
Mar 25 21:37:43.000 [notice] Bootstrapped 100%: Done.
```

Enabling port forwarding

We know that we need to forward port 9001, as it is the ORPort, but we need to know which port the obfsproxy software runs on. This will be logged in the same file and will be discovered by searching the Tor log with the following command:

```
grep obfs3 /var/log/tor/notices.log
```

The previous command should yield the following search result:

```
Mar 05 01:56:04.000 [notice] Registered server transport 'obfs3' at
'0.0.0.0:59519'
```

The obfsproxy port for our obfs3 service is on 59519. From your home router, configure port forwarding from 9001, and configure port forwarding from 59519 from your external IP to BBB. It will also help if you give your BBB a static internal IP. Consult your router's manual for directions. Alternatively, you can specify the port with the following line in the /etc/tor/torrc file:

```
ServerTransportListenAddr obfs3 0.0.0.0:xxxx
```

Replace the x's with the desired port address. However, it's best to let obfsproxy pick a random address; otherwise, the Tor Project might end up with an uneven distribution of bridges running on certain ports, which will make it easier to block access to bridges.

Once you've forwarded the necessary ports, restart the router again. You should see the following messages, indicating success:

```
Mar 25 21:37:43.000 [notice] Now checking whether ORPort xxx.xxx.xxx.
xxx:9001 is reachable... (this may take up to 20 minutes -- look for log
messages indicating success)
Mar 25 21:37:44.000 [notice] Self-testing indicates your ORPort is
reachable from the outside. Excellent. Publishing server descriptor.
```

Congratulations! You are now running a Tor bridge on BBB and are helping to improve Internet freedom. You are also enabling agents, both secret and otherwise, to access the unfiltered Internet.

Adding physical interfaces to the bridge

Now you have a Tor bridge running and you can stop here. If you do, you'd be missing out on the ability to combine software with custom hardware on BBB. Our BBB Tor bridge currently has no visual feedback, so it's not obvious that it's working. Also, the only means to control the bridge is to log in to BBB over SSH and manipulate the configuration options. The Tor bridge is an appliance and it needs appliance controls. In this section, we'll add a front panel, which will give us an easy method to control the bridge's bandwidth and a quick indicator to know that the software hasn't crashed. In the following section, we'll add the software to interface with our bridge and control the hardware.

 If you decide to run a Tor relay, there are websites such as Tor atlas (https://atlas.torproject.org/) that will produce bandwidth graphs and display other information about your relay. Another tool that will also display information about your bridge is Globe (https://globe.torproject.org/).

Gathering the front panel components

As this is our first project, we are going to use some basic components: a **light-emitting diode (LED)**, a rotary potentiometer, and a **liquid-crystal display (LCD)**, all shown in the following circuit diagram:

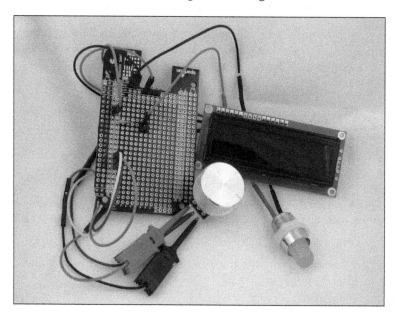

LCDs can been a bit tricky to work with, but SparkFun Electronics has combined a 16x2 LCD with a microcontroller so that it can use a serial interface instead of a more complicated parallel one. The serial interface is simpler because it only requires one data line to the device, whereas a parallel interface will require more wiring.

Using an LCD to display status information

Our Tor bridge generates a lot of metadata, such as the bandwidth usage, the number of connections, and some Tor-specific statistics. For a home network, it's useful to know how much bandwidth your bridge is using, and it would be nice to know this without logging in to BBB all the time. In the serial LCDs, we will draw a graphical representation of the bandwidth usage. We'll use ten bars, each representing a tenth of the available bandwidth. If you see five bars, then the bridge is using half of the available bandwidth. The LCD selected for this project was LCD-09067 (SparkFun Electronics).

SparkFun Electronics is an international distributor that ships products from Boulder, Colorado, in the United States. Some of the more common components recommended in this book can be replaced with equivalent ones in your local electronic store if you are trying to save on shipping. You don't need to type in each component; they are all listed in one consolidated *wish list* at https://www.sparkfun.com/wish_lists/93119.

Controlling the bandwidth with a potentiometer

A potentiometer is like a variable resistor. If you've ever adjusted the volume of a radio or speaker with a knob, you've probably used a potentiometer. By adjusting the knob, you adjust the resistance in the potentiometer, which in turns adjusts the voltage sensed at the output. The potentiometer has three leads: one for voltage (in), one for ground, and the final is the output.

This knob, connected to BeagleBridge, will throttle the bandwidth available to Tor. With the dial turned up to max, the bridge will report that all of your bandwidth is available to route traffic to the Tor network. With the dial at its midpoint, the bridge will report that half of your bandwidth is available for use. If you notice that the bridge is consuming more bandwidth than you'd like, as indicated by the LCD, you can turn down the *volume* of your bridge. The potentiometer and knob for this project are COM-09939 and COM-10001 (SparkFun Electronics).

Your bridge will not immediately attract users; it will take some time. Start with your bridge set at the max bandwidth; if you discover that it is consuming more bandwidth than you like, then turn it down. To receive an indication whether the Tor bridge is working, we will use an LED controlled by a BBB's GPIO, which will flash periodically. This way you can look over at the panel and tell whether the software is still running. The LED by SparkFun is COM-10633, and the LED holder is COM-11148.

Designing the BeagleBridge circuit

The following Fritzing diagram shows the schematic for this project.

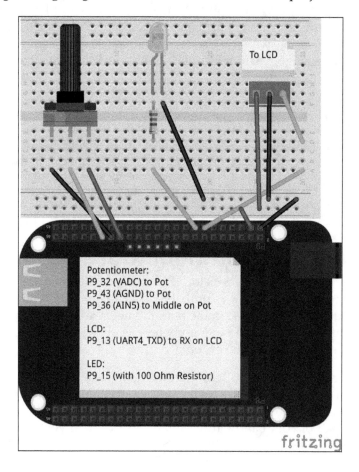

The potentiometer is connected via BBB's **Analog-to-Digital Converter (ADC)** pins. BBB's analog inputs can only tolerate a max of 1.8V; so, it's very important to use the dedicated analog voltage pin, pin P9_32 (pin number 32 of the connector P9), which provides this voltage. Do *not* connect the potentiometer to the normal 3.3V or 5V power rails, as this will damage the processor. We'll arbitrarily pick the analog input AIN5 on pin P9_36 as our input pin, and connect that to the middle lead or output of the potentiometer. Lastly, connect the last lead of the potentiometer to the dedicated analog ground pin, P9_34.

The LED and LCD both use 3.3V and the common ground. We need a serial transmit pin for the LCD, so we'll arbitrarily pick P9_13, which is the transmit for UART4. UART1 transmit on P9_24 or UART2 on P9_21 will also work fine.

Lastly, we need a GPIO to control the LED. Again, any will do, but I've picked pin P9_15. You'll need a resistor to limit the current to the LED. Sizing a resistor is straightforward using Ohm's Law; we just need to know the forward voltage drop and the max current of the LED. This information is found in the datasheet. If you are using SparkFun's 5mm Green LED, its max current is 20mA and has a forward voltage drop of 2.2V.

Ohm's Law states that voltage is equal to the current multiplied by the resistance, or $V = IR$. Subtracting 2.2V from 3.3V of our supply voltage, and dividing the resulting value by .020 Amps gives 55 Ohms. 55 Ohms isn't a standard value, but 56 is, so you can use this. But, you can always use a higher resistance value, and the LED will just be less bright. The resistor used in this project had a value of 100 Ohms.

Wiring the hardware with a proto cape

There are some special considerations when wiring this project as it is meant to go inside an enclosure to provide the front panel. A stranded wire will bend and flex better compared to a solid core. Once settled in the enclosure, we wouldn't expect the wires to strain or move around, but they certainly will when you try to install the panel inside the enclosure! We also have a few options to wire our project to BBB. We could use jumper wires with male pins to insert into the female expansion headers, but these pins can come out easily, especially when you put your project into the enclosure.

We'll use SparkFun's BeagleBone Black Proto Cape, DEV-12774, to easily combine our circuit with BBB. This board breaks out power, ground, and other pin signals for expansion. It includes an EEPROM, which is not only useful if you want to have persistent data stored on your board but is also required if you are building a BeagleBone Cape, which will be discussed in detail in the next chapter. The advantage of a protoboard, especially the Beagle proto capes, is that we can solder male headers on the board and then use female terminated wires, which tend to connect a little better. Plus, by using the male headers, we can easily reuse the protoboard for a later project. However, these protoboards are not required, and if you are trying to save some money, with some creative wiring, you don't need one.

If you are using the protoboard approach, you don't have to populate all the headers either. Only the male pins that we need are soldered to the corresponding pads on the protoboard's P9 header. The way these protoboards work is that each pin is duplicated on the pads next to them. Solder the 100 Ohm resistor from P9_15 to the bottom of one of the male pins in the middle of the board. Then, connect a wire from the male pin to the positive terminal of the LED.

When complete, your project should look something like the following circuit diagram. We don't have the control software running yet, but you can see the LCD displaying the bandwidth usage. The following diagram doesn't have soldered connections to the potentiometer for the ease of testing, but instead uses *IC Hooks*. In a finished installation, you will want to solder the wires for a better mechanical and electrical connection.

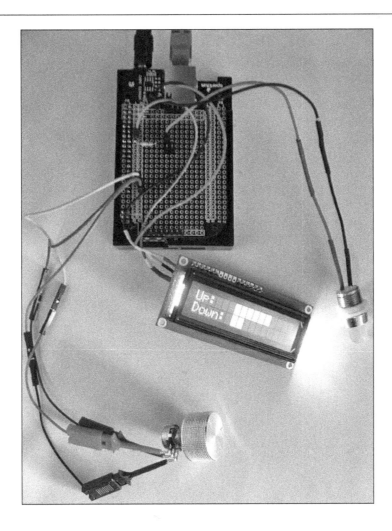

Developing the software using Python libraries

The software for this project is freely available for download at https://github.com/jbdatko/beagle-bone-for-secret-agents/. In this section, we'll highlight the finer details of working with the existing libraries and outline the architecture of the project. The code uses many asynchronous callbacks from these libraries since there are several concurrent activities: the Tor bridge, the bandwidth knob, writing to the LCD, and blinking of the LED. To interact with the bridge, we'll use the Tor Stem library (https://stem.torproject.org/), and to interact with the hardware, we'll use Adafruit's BeagleBone Python library (https://github.com/adafruit/adafruit-beaglebone-io-python).

Controlling the hardware with pyBBIO

We installed the Stem library when we installed Tor; so, now we need to install the Adafruit BBIO library by performing the following commands:

```
sudo apt-get install build-essential python-dev python-setuptools python-pip python-smbus -y
```

```
sudo pip install Adafruit_BBIO
```

```
sudo pip install pyserial
```

The Adafruit library conveniently enables the device tree overlays, which are the files that describe the hardware configuration of BBB to the kernel, at runtime. Therefore, there is no need to manipulate the configuration via the sysfs as everything is handled in the Python library. The code models each hardware component as its own Python class. The LED modeled by the TorFreedomLED class is the most straightforward. We need the LED to blink; this is accomplished by toggling the output high, sleeping the executing thread briefly, and then toggling the output low to turn it off. To set up the GPIO, we only need to call GPIO.setup, by passing in the pin and the direction:

```python
import Adafruit_BBIO.GPIO as GPIO
class TorFreedomLED(object):
  def __init__(self):
    self.pin = 'P9_15'
    GPIO.setup(self.pin, GPIO.OUT)

  def on(self):
    GPIO.output(self.pin, GPIO.HIGH)

  def off(self):
    GPIO.output(self.pin, GPIO.LOW)

  def blink(self):
    self.on()
    sleep(.5)
    self.off()
```

The LCD, controlled by the FrontPanelDisplay class, writes to the serial port, /dev/tty04, on BBB's UART 4 at 9600 baud. The LCD only receives information; therefore, we are only using the transmit lines from BBB. Commands are written to the attached microcontroller, which in turn drives the display. The datasheet, available on the SparkFun website, describes all of the commands. In general, the procedure is to move the virtual cursor on the display and then send the text.

SparkFun has a more complete quick start guide on the serial LCD at
https://www.sparkfun.com/tutorials/246. The example code
is for an Arduino, but porting it to Python is straightforward if you
follow the example of the bridge LCD in this chapter.

Similar to the GPIO example, the serial port in the Adafruit library can be used
as follows:

```python
import Adafruit_BBIO.UART as UART
import serial
class FrontPanelDisplay(object):

    def __init__(self):
        self.uart = 'UART4'
        UART.setup(self.uart)
        self.port = serial.Serial(port="/dev/ttyO4", baudrate=9600)
        self.port.open()
```

The display will automatically wrap lines if the text you are trying to display is
longer than sixteen characters. Therefore, you have to manage the LCD to ensure
that it displays correctly. For example, let's take a look at the display_graph method
that is responsible for producing the bandwidth graph:

```python
self.clear_screen()
up_str = '{0:<16}'.format('Up:    ' + self.block_char * up)
dn_str = '{0:<16}'.format('Down:  ' + self.block_char * down)

self.port.write(up_str)
self.port.write(dn_str)
```

The first line clears the screen and resets the cursor to the top-left corner of the 16x2
display. Next, we format the two lines to display the graph using the special block
character on the LCD. This line is left justified and is filled with whitespace up to
sixteen characters. Finally, the lines are written to the LCD with the serial write
methods. The cursor does not have to be reset between each line because after
writing the first, it will be ready in the second line.

Lastly, the bandwidth adjust knob is modeled in the `BandwidthKnob` class. This class uses the `ADC` module and is also implemented as a thread. The analog input will always produce a value when read, and we will ratio this value to the available bandwidth for the bridge. The `Adafruit` library normalizes the values from `0.0` to `1.0`; so, when the knob is at its midpoint, the call to `ADC.read(pin)` should return `0.5`. There is some jitter in the analog signal, and we don't need a fine resolution on the bandwidth. Sampling once every second should suffice since we don't expect the knob to change frequently. We'll round up to the next whole number, which will give the knob ten discrete settings. The `run` method will report back to the caller, via a message queue, if the *volume* setting has changed. The calling thread can then update the Tor bridge bandwidth limits accordingly.

This code sample shows you how to set up the ADC on BBB with the `Adafruit` library and how to pass that result to a waiting thread with a message queue:

```python
import Adafruit_BBIO.ADC as ADC
import threading
from time import sleep
from math import ceil, floor
import Queue
class BandwidthKnob(threading.Thread):

    def __init__(self, pin, *args, **kwargs):

        threading.Thread.__init__(self, *args, **kwargs)
        self.pin = pin
        self.setup_adc()
        self.kill = False
        self.prev_value = -1
        self.q = Queue.Queue()

    def setup_adc(self):
        'Load the Adafruit device tree fragment for ADC pins'
        ADC.setup()

    def read_value(self):
        return ceil(10 * ADC.read(self.pin))

    def stop(self):
        self.kill = True

    def run(self):
        knob = self.prev_value
```

```
while knob != 0 and not self.kill:
    sleep(1)
    knob = self.read_value()
    if knob != self.prev_value:
        self.q.put(knob)
        self.prev_value = knob
```

Determining your bandwidth with speedtest-cli

In order to adjust the bandwidth rate, we first need to know how much bandwidth our bridge has. Fortunately, there is a nice script to run a speed test from your command line that is appropriately called `speedtest-cli`. This is installed with the following command:

```
sudo pip install git+https://github.com/sivel/speedtest-cli.git
```

Run the test with the following command:

```
speedtest-cli --simple > speedtest.txt
```

If you inspect the output file, you should see something like the following:

```
Ping: 107.686 ms
Download: 28.23 Mbit/s
Upload: 5.37 Mbit/s
```

We'll use the results in this file as the basis for our bandwidth adjustment. At the moment, we only need to remember its location for later use.

Controlling the bridge with the Stem library

The bridge is controlled using the Stem library, which communicates with the Tor process over the Tor control protocol. The setup is managed in the BeagleBridge class. After establishing a connection with the Tor process, this class registers two event listeners for the Bandwidth and Configuration changed event. The bandwidth event is triggered each second and reports, via the print_bw callback, the bytes used in the last second. This information is used to draw the bandwidth graph. The following callback function shows how the callback interacts with the LCD:

```
def make_bw_callback(test,lcd):
    '''Returns a callback function for the bandwidth event'''
    def print_bw(event):
        '''Obtains the bandwidth used from the last second from the
            bridge, normalizes it to the total bandwidth, and draw
            that information to the display'''
        up = int(test.get_up_ratio(event.written))
        down = int(test.get_down_ratio(event.read))
        lcd.display_graph(up, down)

    return print_bw
```

 For those who want to dive deeper into the Stem library and the Tor control protocol, the Stem library has thorough online documentation and examples (https://stem.torproject.org/tutorials. html). The control protocol, for those who want an even more in-depth look, is located at https://gitweb.torproject.org/torspec. git?a=blob_plain;hb=HEAD;f=control-spec.txt.

The Configuration Changed event is the callback to inform the process that the bridge's configuration was changed. This occurs when the bandwidth knob is adjusted, which causes the update_rate method to be called, that sends a command to the bridge to update the configuration. The end result is that by adjusting the knob, you directly affect the bandwidth limits on your bridge. When the callback occurs, it will display the new bandwidth rates on the LCD so that you know that your limit has changed. This callback is shown as follows:

```
def make_conf_callback(lcd):
    '''Returns a callback function for the configuration changed
        event'''
    def conf_changed(event):
        '''Reads the new bandwidth rates from the bridge and draws
```

```
        that information to the display'''
    rate = str(int(event.config['RelayBandwidthRate']) / 1024)
    burst = str(int(event.config['RelayBandwidthBurst']) / 1024)
    lcd.display_rates(rate, burst)

    return conf_changed
```

The main section of the Python script performs the class instantiation and also displays a one-time splash screen to the LCD. It will show the total bytes transmitted by the bridge, the number of established circuits, and the last 24 bytes of the bridge's fingerprint. The bridge controller will run forever, while the bandwidth knob is at a nonzero value. When you dial the knob to zero, the program will exit and the LCD will be filled with blocks.

Finally, to run the bridge controller, execute the following command, with the first parameter being the location of the speed test results:

```
sudo python beaglebridge.py ~/speedtest.txt &
```

To avoid running as root, you'll have to manipulate user groups and permissions. The Tor process runs as the `debian-tor` user, and the `Adafruit` library, which enables device tree overlays on your behalf, needs to run at a user level that has the permission to enable these features. You can create a custom group and a user that is in the `debian-tor` group and then give that group permission to modify the device tree files to not run as root.

Connecting to your obfuscated bridge

With BeagleBridge, you have your own entry point in the Tor network. You can download and install the Tor browser and configure it to use your bridge. This is useful anytime you find yourself on a restricted or hostile network and want to access the Internet more anonymously. However, if you use *your* BeagleBridge, passive attackers could learn the IP address to which you are connecting, which happens to be your home network. The traffic is obfuscated, but it may look suspicious over time. It might be better to use a random bridge address obtained via Tor. Even if you don't directly connect to your own bridge, your bridge is helping to contribute resources to the Tor network, which helps everybody access a censor-free Internet. To connect to your bridge, launch the Tor browser and click on **Open Settings** as it starts up. Then, answer with a `Yes` to questions about whether your connection is censored. Select **Enter Custom Bridges** and enter your bridge as follows, but replace the x's with your IP address and the port number of your bridge:

```
bridge obfs3 XXX.XXX.XXX.XXX:59519
```

Continuing with Tor-related projects

This project is just the first step in learning Tor. If you want to route more traffic with BBB, you can switch from a bridge to a public relay. Relays receive more traffic but are also more public. Your IP address will be listed as a public bridge, and some websites will refuse to serve you content even if you are running a nonexit relay.

You can also run a Tor **hidden service** on the BeagleBone. Using Tor with a client helps to anonymize your IP address to a server, but a Tor hidden service hides the server's IP address from a client. It would be an interesting project for a BeagleBone if you had a service that you want accessible only through Tor.

Hardware-wise, consider placing the BeagleBone and front panel in a dedicated enclosure. See whether there is a local hackerspace around you, and they may be able to help you make a nice laser-cut enclosure! If you don't have a laser cutter, you can use a SparkFun Electronics box like the one in the following screenshot:

 The onion logo is a registered trademark of the Tor Project, used with permission. The BeagleBridge project described in this chapter is not affiliated to the Tor Project.

Summary

In this chapter, you learned about Tor and how to circumvent Internet censorship by running a Tor bridge on BBB. We've also shown how to add some basic hardware controls to BBB in order to create a front panel interface. Lastly, through some Python code, we were able to tie the hardware controls and the Tor bridge together.

In the next chapter, we'll take a closer look at specialized cryptographic hardware available for BBB and show you how to use each of these devices.

3

Adding Hardware Security with the CryptoCape

This chapter continues our custom security hardware journey by using a **BeagleBone Black (BBB) cape**. In BeagleBone parlance, a **cape** is a daughterboard that attaches to the BBB. We'll briefly introduce hardware cryptographic devices and then explore the CryptoCape, which is a BBB cape containing numerous security features. We'll describe the process of creating your own cape using the CryptoCape as an example. This chapter introduces the crypto chips on the cape and shows you how to implement a biometric authentication device using the CryptoCape and a fingerprint scanner.

This chapter will discuss the following topics:

- The pros and cons of hardware-based cryptography
- An overview of the CryptoCape
- How cape EEPROMs enable automatic hardware configuration on the BBB
- How to use the CryptoCape's real-time clock
- How to program an ATmega328p from BBB
- How to implement a biometric authentication system

Exploring the differences between hardware and software cryptography

In the following sections, we'll discuss the advantages and disadvantages of using hardware-based cryptography. The remaining projects in the book will use embedded hardware cryptographic devices, so it's important to know their capabilities and their limitations. Refer to *Chapter 1, Creating Your BeagleBone Black Development Environment*, for additional resources on cryptography and terms used in this section.

Understanding the advantages of hardware-based cryptography

For the advantages of hardware cryptography, we'll focus on the embedded environment since that is the target use case of BBB. While chip manufacturers may provide a laundry list of advantages, there are two main categories: cryptographic acceleration and key isolation features.

Offloading computation to a separate processor

One advantage of using a dedicated cryptographic co-processor is to offload computation to reduce CPU usage. A typical example is using hardware to perform the **Advanced Encryption Standard** (**AES**) encryption and decryption operations in a **Transport Layer Security** (**TLS**) session.

TLS is most commonly used in conjunction with the **Hypertext Transfer Protocol Secure** (**HTTPS**) protocol. You use HTTPS every time you buy something online to protect your credit card information. Depending on your browser, you may notice a lock icon or a green bar to indicate when a web page is served over HTTPS. In a TLS session, the client, your browser, and the server will negotiate to use the same symmetric key. While there are several symmetric ciphers that can be negotiated, AES is one of the preferred choices.

 While some sites automatically redirect you to the HTTPS version of the site, often you must manually specify this. Remembering to type `https://` is often annoying but fortunately there is a cross-browser plugin that will automatically redirect you to the HTTPS site, if there is one. The plugin is called **HTTPS Everywhere** and it is maintained by the Electronic Frontier Foundation. Information and links to download the free software are located at `https://www.eff.org/https-everywhere`.

In the crypto accelerator role, a cryptographic co-processor would perform the encryption and decryption of each TLS record. This offloads the main CPU to handle the processing of the network traffic and perform the intended application. The BBB actually has such a cryptographic co-processor. **Texas Instruments** (**TI**) crypto performance page for the AM335x, the processor on the BBB, shows the results of their benchmark tests with OpenSSL. Using AES with a 256 bit key size and operating on blocks of 8192 bytes, the measured throughput of data was 8129.19 kB/sec without using crypto acceleration. This test resulted in a CPU usage of 69 percent. However, using the crypto co-processor on the AM335x, they measured a throughput of 24376.66 kB/sec with a CPU usage of 41 percent. That's almost a 200 percent gain in throughput performance and a 40 percent drop in CPU usage!

More information on the crypto accelerators on the AM335x can be found on TI Crypto Performance page at `http://processors.wiki.ti.com/index.php/AM335x_Crypto_Performance`.

If your embedded application's purpose is to perform a computationally intense calculation, using a cryptographic co-processor designed to offload the crypto processing can save your CPU cycles for your main program.

Protecting keys through physical isolation

A major advantage of using hardware cryptography devices is that keys can be generated internal to the device and are designed to be difficult to remove. In the web server world, these devices are called **Hardware Security Modules** (**HSMs**). In April 2014, a major vulnerability was announced that affected the OpenSSL software, colloquially called **heartbleed**. The vulnerability was not a cryptographic one *per se*, but rather the result of a programming error called a **buffer overrun**. This vulnerability is unfortunately common in the C programming language, in which OpenSSL is written, because of the lack of automatic array bounds checking. It was possible for a client to exploit this error and view internal memory of the server, potentially discovering sensitive information. The code to fix this problem was shorter than this paragraph.

 The following `xkcd` comic provides a succinct and amusing explanation of the heartbleed bug:
`https://xkcd.com/1354/`

The scale and severity of this vulnerability cannot be overstated. The most damaging attack is if the server's private key was leaked. Knowing the private key, an attacker can impersonate the server, and clients could willingly disclose private information to the impostor. However, on a server with a HSM, the heartbleed vulnerability was more limited. Sensitive information, such as session cookies, would still have leaked via the software exploit. Yet the server's private key, which remains in the HSM, would not have leaked.

Since the hardware cryptographic co-processor runs as a physically separate machine, it is very difficult for software exploits running on the main processor to disclose secrets in the hardware module. In the embedded world, there are several chips that perform this key isolation feature.

Understanding the disadvantages of hardware crypto devices

Adding hardware cryptographic devices doesn't automatically make your project *secure*. In the following sections, we'll discuss some of the downsides to using cryptographic hardware and some of the concerns you would need to resolve when using them in your project.

Lacking cryptographic flexibility

A hardware cryptographic device is generally not configurable. This is usually by design but the implication is that it is difficult, if not impossible, to alter the cryptographic behavior of the device. If you select a chip that performs encryption with a limited key size, you will not be able to upgrade the device with a stronger key size later. It is generally easier to update software-based encryption systems.

Exposing hardware-specific attack vectors

While an isolated crypto processor may reduce attacks or exploits from the software, it often allows more sophisticated hardware-based attacks. There are three categories of hardware-based attacks: noninvasive, invasive, and semi-invasive (Skoroboga, 2011). Noninvasive attacks treat the chip as a black box and attempt to manipulate the surrounding environment to perform an exploit. Successful non-invasive attacks include performing a **Differential Power Analysis (DPA)** to monitor the chip as it performs an encryption algorithm. By measuring the power usage during the encryption operation, it is possible to see the key through distinct power signatures. An invasive attack usually involves physically destroying the chip in some manner to gain access to its internals. Semi-invasive attacks may involve some sort of laser imaging to observe or interfere with the chip.

To perform a glitch attack, an attack attempts to manipulate the executing instruction by injecting a fault (Bar-El, 2004). Colin O'Flynn, a security researcher, has a concise and clear example of how a glitch attack can cause a password-checking microprocessor to fail: https://www.youtube.com/watch?v=Ruphw9-8JWE&list=UUqc9MJwX_R1pQC6A353JmJg.

Obfuscating implementation details

A final consideration is that while chip vendors may publish the interface to their device, the internals are often proprietary. This is similar to a software vendor who publishes the software programming interface, but provides only the compiled binary and not the source code. In this case, the chip is treated as a black box, and without a mechanism to verify the device, you have to trust that it is operating correctly. As cryptographic libraries are ported to unique microcontrollers by the open source community, this situation will hopefully improve.

Summarizing the hardware versus software debate

So, which is the better route? As with most complex technologies the correct answer is: *it depends*. For a truly embedded system, one that can't spare even a few extra bytes, a hardware security chip may be your only option if you can't upgrade your microprocessor. Also, if there is a high threat of leaking your key due to a software vulnerability, then the separate crypto co-processor might help you. However, if an attacker can gain physical access to your device, then they might be able to extract the key with hardware-based attacks. Lastly, if transparency is paramount for you to verify the lack or existence of backdoors, then only fully open source software and hardware devices will satisfy you.

Touring the CryptoCape

The CryptoCape is BeagleBone's first dedicated security daughterboard. As the BBB already has cryptographic accelerations, the chips on the CryptoCape provide the *key isolation* features discussed in the previous section. In the BeagleBone community, daughterboards are called *capes* which are analogous to Arduino *shields*. The CryptoCape contains several crypto ICs that you may use in your projects. The design is open source hardware, so you may also visit the SparkFun website to retrieve the design files. The CryptoCape contains the following major components:

Component	Manufacturer	Features
AT97SC3205T	Atmel	TPM — RSA 2048 encryption and SHA1 hashing
ATAES132	Atmel	Encrypted EEPROM with AES-128-CCM
ATSHA204	Atmel	SHA-2 hashing (SHA-256, HMAC-256)
ATECC108	Atmel	ECDSA with NIST curves

Component	Manufacturer	Features
ATmega328p	Atmel	Microcontroller
DS3231M	Maxim integrated	Real-time clock with battery
CAT24C256	ON semiconductor	EEPROM

If you imagine the BBB's Ethernet connector as a neck, then it appears that the cutouts of the attached daughterboard seem to wrap around it as if it were wearing a cape, hence the name. Also, Boris, the beagle mascot of BeagleBoard.org, looks more adorable in a cape.

Each of these chips and the associated circuits are clearly labeled on the CryptoCape board:

In the following sections, we'll briefly introduce each component and provide some example project ideas.

Discovering the I2C protocol

Every chip on the CryptoCape uses the **Inter-Integrated Circuit** (**I2C**) Bus. I2C was developed by Phillips Semiconductor over 20 years ago, but it is still very prevalent in electronics design today. I2C requires two signal lines, one for a **Serial Clock** (**SCL**) and the other for **Serial Data** (**SDA**). Devices attached to the bus are either classified as master or slave. Each slave device has an address and there can be more than one master. The I2C protocol supports collision detection and is a true multimaster protocol.

The SDA and SCL lines are *pulled up* to the system voltage, VCC, typically with resistors connected from VCC to SDA and VCC to SCL. The processor on the BBB, the AM335x, contains internal pull-up resistors for the bus. Data is encoded to the bus by manipulating the logic levels of the SDA and SCL lines. For example, to start sending data, the master pulls SDA low while holding SCL at a logic high. The stop condition is sent with a low to high transition of SDA while holding SCL high.

 Revision 6 of the I2C bus specification can be found on NXP semiconductors (previously Phillips) website at http://www.nxp. com/documents/user_manual/UM10204.pdf.

The following screenshot shows a normal I2C operation as captured by a logic analyzer. A **logic analyzer** is an instrument that can sample electrical connections and often decode the signals to produce a human readable format.

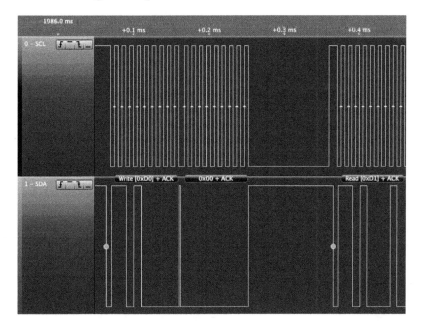

Understanding the benefit of cape EEPROMs

At a glance, the CAT24C256 **Electrically Erasable Programmable Read Only Memory (EEPROM)** doesn't appear to add much value to the board. After all, the BeagleBone has a 2GB eMMC on the early revisions and a 4GB eMMC on revision C. An extra 256 kB of memory is hardly food scraps for the beagle. However, it serves a greater purpose; it's what enables automatic cape detection by the BBB.

The BBB has two 46 pin female expansion ports offering much more I/O capabilities than any other hobbyist board on the market. Certain pins can actually support eight different modes, mode 0 through mode 7. The mapping of pin features to a mode is known as **pin muxing**, short for pin multiplexing. To use a pin in a certain mode, the software must enable and configure this pin through the kernel's interface. This can be manually performed or scripted, but the easiest method is to use a BeagleBone cape.

During the kernel startup, the software will probe the I2C bus looking for cape EEPROMs. There are four valid addresses for Cape EEPROMs, 0x54 through 0x57. Therefore, the BBB supports up to four attached capes. The BBB will read the cape EEPROM, which must be programmed using the format in the BBB **System Reference Manual (SRM)**. The BBB, using a software package called the **capemgr**, short for **Cape Manager**, will read the board name and revision from the Cape EEPROM. It will then try to match the name and revision to a compiled device tree fragment on your BBB. If there is a match, it will load that fragment.

 The latest production files for the BBB including the schematics and the SRM are located on the BBB wiki at `http://elinux.org/Beagleboard:BeagleBoneBlack`.

This automatic configuration provides two benefits. The first is that the pins on the BBB are automatically configured for a cape. The second is that the device tree can specify the kernel driver for the hardware on the cape, which means that the drivers for your hardware can be automatically loaded. The `capemgr` provides a plug-and-play like experience for embedded Linux.

If you are developing a BeagleBone cape, you should consider the process to have your cape supported in the BeagleBone images. This is a three-step process. First, you need to create a cape EEPROM file. This file should be written to your cape at manufacturing time. Second, you need to create a **Device Tree Source** (DTS) file, following the cape naming convention previously discussed, and submit a pull request on GitHub to BeagleBoard.org. Lastly, you need to create an eLinux wiki site discussing your cape. In the next sections, we'll briefly describe the software and hardware required to build a BeagleBone cape using the CryptoCape as an example.

Creating a cape EEPROM

If you have any semi-complicated hardware for the BeagleBone, you will benefit by adding a cape-compatible EEPROM. The essential reference to populating the EEPROM is the BeagleBone SRM's section on *Cape Board Support*. This section contains the EEPROM format. To jumpstart your EEPROM file creation, you can use a tool called the **EEPROM cape generator** available at: `https://github.com/picoflamingo/BBCape_EEPROM`. This tool with its simple command-line interface will provide the skeleton for your cape EEPROM. Currently, it does not completely implement the cape specification, so you must use a binary editor to set the remaining values of the EEPROM. The process to create the EEPROM binary involves reading through the SRM and writing the appropriate values, at the correct offsets, in a binary file.

You can view the CryptoCape's EEPROM by executing the following command as root:

```
cat /sys/bus/i2c/devices/1-0057/eeprom | hexdump -C
```

By default, the CryptoCape EEPROM is located at address 0x57 on the I2C bus. If you have multiple capes, you can change the address of the CryptoCape EEPROM by placing a solder jumper or solder *blob* on the A0 or A1 address pads next to the EEPROM. The results of reading the EEPROM with the previous command will produce the following:

```
00000000  aa 55 33 ee 41 31 42 42  2d 42 4f 4e 45 2d 43 52
          |.U3.A1BB-BONE-CR|
00000010  59 50 54 4f 00 00 00 00  00 00 00 00 00 00 00 00
          |YPTO............|
00000020  00 00 00 00 00 00 30 30  41 30 53 70 61 72 6b 46
          |......00A0SparkF|
00000030  75 6e 00 00 00 00 00 00  00 00 42 42 2d 42 4f 4e
          |un........BB-BON|
00000040  45 2d 43 52 59 50 54 4f  00 00 00 11 32 30 31 34
```

```
           |E-CRYPTO....2014|
00000050   30 30 30 30 30 30 30 30   00 00 00 00 00 00 00 00
           |00000000........|
00000060   00 00 00 00 00 00 00 00   00 00 e0 73 e0 73 00 00
           |..........s.s..|
00000070   00 00 00 00 00 00 00 00   00 00 00 00 a0 26 c0 06
           |.............&..|
00000080   00 00 00 00 00 00 00 00   00 00 00 00 00 00 00 00
           |................|
00000090   00 00 a0 2f 00 00 00 00   00 00 c0 17 00 00 00 00
           |.../............|
000000a0   00 00 00 00 00 00 00 00   00 00 00 00 00 00 00 00
           |................|
*
000000e0   00 00 00 00 00 00 00 00   00 00 00 00 01 f4 00 00
           |................|
000000f0   00 00 00 00 47 50 47 20   46 69 6e 67 65 72 70 72
           |....GPG Fingerpr|
00000100   69 6e 74 3a 20 30 78 42   35 39 31 39 42 31 41 43
           |int: 0xB5919B1AC|
00000110   37 31 33 35 39 30 35 46   34 36 36 39 43 38 34 37
           |7135905F4669C847|
00000120   42 46 41 35 30 33 31 42   44 32 45 44 45 41 36 0a
           |BFA5031BD2EDEA6.|
00000130   ff ff ff ff ff ff ff ff   ff ff ff ff ff ff ff ff
           |................|
*
00008000
```

If you walk through the SRM EEPROM data format, you should be able to match the fields with those in the CryptoCape EEPROM. The two most important fields are the Board Name, which starts at offset 6 and is 32 bytes in length and the Version, which starts at byte 38 and is 4 bytes in length. From the previous example, the board name is BB-BONE-CRYPTO and the version is 00A0. These two components are needed to name the DTS file in the next section. Starting at offset 244, the manufacturer can place any nonvolatile information. The CryptoCape contains the **GNU Privacy Guard** (GPG) fingerprint of the author's GPG public key, which is used to sign software packages and e-mail. In your cape, you could populate this with initial values for software or something similar.

Creating the cape DTS file

Besides the EEPROM, you will also need to create a DTS file. This file defines attributes of your hardware to the Linux kernel. The DTS file for the CryptoCape Revision 00A0 is located on GitHub at: `https://github.com/beagleboard/linux/blob/3.8/firmware/capes/BB-BONE-CRYPTO-00A0.dts`. When creating a new DTS for your hardware, it's best to review the existing BeagleBone DTS files. With the growing number of capes, there is a good chance that there exists an approved DTS file with the hardware configuration you seek.

The BBB device tree overlay system is one of the areas undergoing active development, and important technical nuances change rapidly. If you need to build your own DTS file, it's best to check in with the BeagleBoard.org mailing list available at `https://groups.google.com/forum/#!forum/beagleboard`.

 A detailed introduction to the device tree system in the Linux kernel was presented by Thomas Petazzoni at the Embedded Linux Conference Europe in November 2013. The presentation is available on YouTube at `https://www.youtube.com/watch?v=m_NyYEBxfn8`.

Let's briefly look at a portion of the CryptoCape's DTS file. The `capemgr` will load the compiled version of this file to configure the hardware. The drivers for some of the chips on the CryptoCape are also loaded automatically since they are specified in the DTS file, as shown in the following code:

```
fragment@2 {
        target = <&i2c2>;

        __overlay__ {
          #address-cells = <1>;
          #size-cells = <0>;

          /* Real Time Clock */
          ds1307@68 {
            compatible = "ds1307";
            reg = <0x68>;
          };

          /* TPM   */
          tpm_i2c_atmel@29 {
            compatible = "tpm_i2c_atmel";
            reg = <0x29>;
          };
        };
    };
```

The previous code snippet loads two kernel drivers for two devices on the I2C bus. The first is the RTC at address 0x68. The DS3231M is compatible with the `ds1307` driver. The second is the TPM driver, `tpm_i2c_atmel`, which is located at address 0x29. The EEPROM driver is automatically loaded and the other chips currently do not have a native Linux kernel driver.

If you have your DTS file completed and want it included in the official BBB image, you can submit a pull request to the previously mentioned repository that contains the CryptoCape DTS file. Since this repository contains the existing DTS files for the BeagleBone firmware, it is well worth studying if you are building your own cape.

Creating an eLinux wiki site

The last step is to create a Wiki site on `eLinux.org` and e-mail `support@circuitco.com` to let them know to link it to the main BeagleBone Capes page. The page is the main site for all BeagleBone capes and it is where the community expects to find cape information. The CryptoCape page, with links to all the supporting software and datasheet is located at `http://elinux.org/Cryptotronix:CryptoCape`.

The EEPROM is the defining cape component. Even if you don't manufacture a cape, you can still benefit from adding the EEPROM and creating the DTS files for your own design to take advantage of the BeagleBone's automatic hardware configuration.

Keeping time with a real-time clock

Having all clocks synchronized throughout a system is often an assumption that doesn't hold for embedded devices. Specialized devices may not need to know the time to perform their function. However, in security protocols, accurate time keeping is often important. For example, in TLS, the X.509 certificates that are used to prove the identity of web servers contain a validity range. There is a *not before* and *not after* time that specifies when that certificate is valid. Without an accurate time keeping system, a device can't enforce this date range allowing it to possibly accept expired or not yet valid certificates.

If you use your BBB in an offline environment, but still need accurate time, then you can insert a coin cell battery into the battery compartment of the CryptoCape. When the BBB is disconnected from power, the RTC will receive enough power from the battery to maintain accurate time.

The BBB already contains an RTC; however, it lacks a dedicated battery. It is possible to power the entire BBB from a battery using the battery access pads located near the DC barrel plug adapter; however, a greater capacity battery would be needed since the entire board is powered from these pads.

The RTC driver is loaded automatically, which you can verify by running:

```
dmesg | grep rtc
```

This should result in the following:

```
[    0.729101] omap_rtc 44e3e000.rtc: rtc core: registered 44e3e000.rtc
as rtc0
[    0.748605] rtc-ds1307 1-0068: rtc core: registered ds1307 as rtc1
[    0.748627] rtc-ds1307 1-0068: 56 bytes nvram
[    0.977426] [drm] Cannot find any crtc or sizes - going 1024x768
[    1.048851] omap_rtc 44e3e000.rtc: setting system clock to 2000-01-01
00:00:01 UTC (946684801)
```

The previous example shows the BBB's RTC, omap_rtc, registered as rtc0 and the not-so-accurate-time of 2000-01-01 being set. The CryptoCape's RTC is rtc1 and the time value is not manipulated.

You will have to set the RTC time initially after installing the CryptoCape. First, you'll need an accurate system time. Refer to the project from *Chapter 2, Circumventing Censorship with a Tor Bridge*, on how this is done. Set the RTC from the system time with the following command:

```
hwclock -w -f /dev/rtc1
```

Cross-check the time to ensure it was set properly:

```
hwclock -r -f /dev/rtc1
```

This should produce something like the following:

```
Tue 13 May 2014 07:29:27 PM UTC  -0.198319 seconds
```

If you use the coin cell battery from SparkFun Electronics, it has a stated capacity of 47mAh. The DS3231m draws 2 *micro* Amps when on the battery. Ideally, this would result in 23,500 hours of run time on the battery or about 2.7 *years*. In actuality, you see much less run time from your battery, but even if the battery dies in half of the ideal time, you should still see plenty of battery life from your RTC.

Trusting computing devices with a Trusted Platform Module

The **Trusted Platform Module (TPM)** performs the RSA algorithm on the chip. However, it is much more capable than just an encryption chip. The TPM specification is developed and maintained by the **Trusted Computing Group (TCG)**, an international industry standards body.

TPMs are included on several major vendor laptops including Dell, HP, and even Google Chromebooks. On laptops, TPMs are normally found in the **Low Pin Count (LPC)** package and are enabled via the BIOS. Embedded devices typically don't support the LPC bus; the TPM on the CryptoCape communicates over the I2C bus.

The software interface to the TPM is via the **Trusted Computing Group Software Stack (TSS)**. In Linux, the TSS is provided by the TrouSerS package. In the next chapter, we'll be using the TPM and also take a closer look at the TPM on the CryptoCape.

Providing hardware authentication with ATSHA204 and ATECC108

Both ATSHA204 and ATECC108 are authentication devices. **Authentication** is the process of guaranteeing the identity of communicating parties and ensuring data integrity. Each chip uses a different approach to authentication. The ATECC108 device uses elliptical curve cryptography to provide the **Elliptical Curve Digital Signature Algorithm (ECDSA)**. The ATSHA024 device uses a hash algorithm, SHA-256, to provide **Hash Based Message Authentication Codes (HMAC)**.

 These two devices are not used in this book, but you can download the software from https://github.com/cryptotronix/hashlet and https://github.com/cryptotronix/eclet and see the example usage for ATSHA204 and ATECC108 respectively.

Encrypting EEPROM data with the ATAES132

The ATAES132 is a 32kb EEPROM that can be encrypted with AES using a 128-bit key using the **Counter with CBC-MAC (CCM)** mode. CCM provides an authenticated encryption mode. With an encrypted EEPROM, you can store small amounts of data-at-rest more securely. The ATAES132 also has the ability to encrypt and decrypt small packets of up to 32 bytes and return the result over the bus. The AES key remains in the device at all times.

At the time of writing this, there isn't a Linux driver for the ATAES132 device, but Atmel provides full documentation and an AVR-based library on their website at `http://www.atmel.com/devices/ataes132.aspx`.

Combining the BBB with an ATmega328p

Lastly, the CryptoCape contains an independent microcontroller. This microcontroller is the **ATmega328p**, which is the same microcontroller on the Arduino UNO. However, because the supply voltage is 3.3V and not 5V like the Arduino UNO, the processor runs at a clock speed of 8MHz versus 16Mhz. In this sense, it is more like the 3.3V Arduino Pro Mini. Shipped from SparkFun, the CryptoCape contains the 3.3V Arduino Pro Mini bootloader. Like any other Arduino-based board, you can reflash the bootloader by attaching an **In-System Programming (ISP)** programmer to the ISP headers next to the ATmega328p. SparkFun's pocket programmer is an inexpensive tool to perform this task. Just be sure to set the switch to *no power target* since the CryptoCape is powered from the BBB.

While you can use an ISP programmer, you can also use the BBB as a programmer. The BBB contains both serial UART and SPI; however, only the serial UART, UART 4, is connected to the onboard ATmega328p. Like the Arduino UNO, if the microprocessor is reset, it will accept uploaded programs over the serial line.

A simple script that toggles the BBB GPIO connected to ATmega's reset line, which is GPIO 49 for the CryptoCape, and then uploads the hex file using `avrdude` will do the trick. The script is part of a GitHub repository which can be cloned with the command:

```
git clone https://github.com/jbdatko/BBB_ATmega328P_flasher.git
```

In this repository, there is an `upload.sh` script, the main logic of which contains the following code snippet:

```
(echo 0 > /sys/class/gpio/gpio49/value \
    && sleep $tts \
```

```
        && echo 1 > \
        /sys/class/gpio/gpio49/value) &

    avrdude -c arduino -p m328p -b 57600 -v \
        -P /dev/ttyO4 -U flash:w:$1
```

The first part toggles the ATmega reset line low and sleeps for $tts, which is currently defined to be .9 seconds. Then the script sets the reset line back to high to let the ATmega run. The next line is the avrdude command to upload your hex file. You'll need to install avrdude with the following command:

sudo apt-get install avrdude

Then, to run the script, perform the following:

sudo ./upload Blink.cpp.hex

Prior to flashing an Arduino sketch, you must have a sketch to flash. Depending on your development preference, there are several options. You can build your AVR program on the BBB with a makefile and gcc-avr. Or you can build your program with Atmel's free AVR Studio or the Arduino IDE. Whichever way you choose, you need to find the compiled hex file and download it to the BBB using sftp or a similar tool.

Before you upload sketches to the CryptoCape's ATmega, you'll need to perform one very important step: you need to attach jumpers to the two *Program Jumper* pins. Without the jumpers, the ATmega is not electrically connected to the BBB serial lines. This is a security feature. Using the Arduino bootloader, it is possible to upload hex files using serial UART. Thus, with the jumpers installed, the sketch on the CryptoCape's ATmega can always be modified. Now imagine if the BBB was inflicted with malware, but had the jumpers removed. This malware can't change the software on the ATmega. It can still do lots of other nasty things including resetting the ATmega, but it can't upload new firmware unless the jumpers are attached.

Building a two-factor biometric system

With an independent processor on the CryptoCape, we can create some interesting applications. Since the ATmega cannot be flashed from the BeagleBone unless the physical jumpers are attached to the board, we can consider this to be a *trusted* processor. In this project, we'll implement a biometric authentication system with a fingerprint sensor and the CryptoCape. We'll use the ATmega to prevent access to the security ICs on the CryptoCape until you have authenticated yourself *to the ATmega* with your fingerprint.

A notable example of fingerprint biometrics in consumer devices is Apple's Touch ID technology on the iPhone 5s. The sensor used on the iPhone is much more sophisticated and expensive than the sensor we will use in this project. But by performing this project, you should appreciate the capabilities and challenges of using biometric technologies. On the Touch ID support page, Apple motivates the use of the technology with the argument that unlocking the phone with your fingerprint is more secure than having no passcode and easier than entering a code each time. In a later section, we'll discuss the weakness of biometric systems.

The major components needed for this project are listed in the following table. The SparkFun parts are listed as they were the ones used, but feel free to substitute equivalent components. The CryptoCape, which is only manufactured by SparkFun Electronics, is open source hardware and the board design files are licensed under a Creative Commons license, so you could also make your own CryptoCape if you wish. You will also need a basic soldering station and appropriate accessories.

Component	SparkFun SKU
Fingerprint sensor	SEN-11792
CryptoCape	DEV-12773
JST jumper wire assembly	PRT-10359
Female jumper wires	PRT-11710
Male breakaway headers	PRT-00116
2-pin jumpers	PRT-09044

The following components are optional, but are nice to have:

Component	SparkFun SKU
Heat shrink kit	PRT-09353
Third hand	TOL-09317
Heaterizer XL-3000	TOL-10326

The fingerprint sensor overview

The Fingerprint sensor is the GT-511C3 device from ADH Technology. This device contains an optical sensor for reading the fingerprints but also an ARM Cortex M3 processor for computing the image recognition. The interface to this device is via serial UART, using 3.3V level logic, and at a baud rate of 9600 bps. There are four wires to connect from the JST connector: transmit, receive, GND, and power.

The datasheet states that the false acceptance rate is less than .001 percent and the false rejection rate is less than .1 percent. In short, this is a very capable fingerprint sensor. The fingerprint data is analyzed and stored on this device. We will use an existing library to communicate with this hardware.

Appreciating the limitations of fingerprint biometrics

Realize that this fingerprint sensor authentication mechanism is only as strong as your fingerprint. A common critic against using fingerprint sensors centers around the fact that it is difficult for you to change your fingerprint. Once your fingerprint is copied you can't revoke or change it as you can with a password. Using a fingerprint as a two-factor mechanism slightly reduces the risk of an authentication breach since a pin or password is still required. You can also mitigate the risk of a fake fingerprint attack on your sensor by stationing an armed guard to watch the sensor as Bruce Schneier, a security technologist, stated in a September 2013 opinion article in WIRED magazine. Such luxuries are often limited to deep-pocketed governments.

Mythbusters, a popular science and engineering program on the Discovery Channel, busted the myth that fingerprints could not be copied and showed how to defeat fingerprint sensors: `https://www.youtube.com/watch?v=3Hji3kp_i9k`. Also, days after the Apple iPhone 5s was released, the biometrics hacking team of the **Chaos Computer Club (CCC)** showed how to bypass the fingerprint sensor: `http://www.ccc.de/en/updates/2013/ccc-breaks-apple-touchid`.

Perhaps the greatest danger of biometric systems is the potential for a grave privacy breach. A database of fingerprints should be well protected since once the fingerprints are exposed they are no longer useful for any other biometric system, *ever*. In August 2014, Hold Security, an information security forensics company, reported to the *New York Times* that over 1.2 billion usernames and passwords were acquired by a Russian crime organization. While incredibly damaging, this breach would be irrecoverable if fingerprint biometrics were used. Hopefully, companies aren't storing fingerprints directly but representations of the fingerprint similar to a hash digest. However, if implemented poorly, the results can be as disastrous as storing the raw fingerprint.

With these warnings in mind, we will continue with using a fingerprint sensor for this project. You'll gain insight on how a fingerprint sensor works and how to it fits into an authentication system. When you are finished with this project, however, you should probably delete your fingerprint from the sensor's database.

Preparing the CryptoCape

In order to make the CryptoCape more *hackable*, we need to populate the pads attached to the I/O signals with male headers. This will allow us to connect various external components. While you could directly solder to the pads, it's best if you solder a male 0.1" pin, which will allow you to easily connect a female terminated wire for your project, which can then be reused.

A fully populated CryptoCape will look like the following image. A strip of breakaway headers of 31 pins or more will be enough to populate each pad. Technically, you don't need to populate the EEPROM write protect pads unless you want to write to the EEPROM. However, if you overwrite the EEPROM cape information, the BBB might not load the correct drivers.

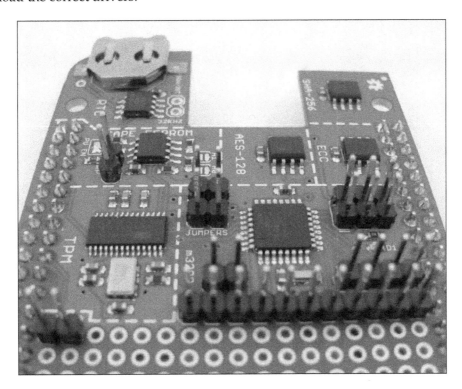

Preparing the connections

Before attaching any connections, we physically need a method to attach the ends of the JST cable to the CryptoCape. The CryptoCape has 0.1" pads, which will fit 0.1" male headers and female-to-female jumper wires fit nicely to that connection. One end of the JST connector is simply four bare wires. If you solder each of these wires to a 4x1 0.1" male header, you can make a simple connector. Using a third hand, you can solder the JST wires to the headers and for a finishing touch, add heat-shrink around the wire and the male pin. Just remember to put your heat shrink on before you solder! The completed connector should look something like this:

Connecting the Scanner to the CryptoCape

We'll attach the fingerprint scanner to the CryptoCape. The Arduino compatible library for this sensor was developed by Josh Hawley. This library is configured to use digital pin 4 for the receive pin on the ATmega and digital pin 5 as the transmit pin from the ATmega. These pins are appropriately labeled *D4* and *D5* on the CryptoCape, just under the ATmega. The remaining two pins are 3.3V power and ground which are also on the same row as the D4 and D5 pins. Attach the female ends of the jumper wires to these pins. If you are using the SparkFun JST connector, the pins from the fingerprint scanner are in the following order, starting with the black wire: D4, D5, GND, Power.

Preparing the fingerprint sensor

The fingerprint sensor must be trained to recognize your fingerprint through a process called **enrollment**. There are several methods to enroll your fingerprint. The SparkFun website has instructions on how to use the ADH-Tech provided Windows-based software to program the sensor. However, you'll need an extra component, that is, the FTDI Basic Breakout board to convert USB from your computer to serial for the scanner. You could also use an Arduino directly, but you must also use logic level converters if you are using a 5V Arduino. Since the CryptoCape has an Arduino compatible processor, we will show you how to do this with your BBB and CryptoCape. The repository that contains the ATmega firmware can be cloned on your BBB with the following command:

```
git clone https://github.com/jbdatko/Fingerprint_Scanner-TTL.git
```

In this repository, the FPS_Enroll.ino file will enroll, or add, a fingerprint to the sensor's database. As previously mentioned, you'll need to compile this file out of band. Alternatively, you can use the pre-compiled version in the repository above.

Upload the enroll script:

```
sudo ./upload.sh FPS_Enroll.cpp.hex
```

You should see text scroll by that looks like this:

```
Reading | ############################################## | 100% 0.00s

avrdude: Device signature = 0x1e950f
avrdude: safemode: lfuse reads as 0
avrdude: safemode: hfuse reads as 0
avrdude: safemode: efuse reads as 0
avrdude: NOTE: FLASH memory has been specified, an erase cycle will be
performed
        To disable this feature, specify the -D option.
avrdude: erasing chip
avrdude: reading input file "FPS_Enroll.cpp.hex"
avrdude: input file FPS_Enroll.cpp.hex auto detected as Intel Hex
avrdude: writing flash (11458 bytes):

Writing | ############################################## | 100% 3.09s

avrdude: 11458 bytes of flash written
avrdude: verifying flash memory against FPS_Enroll.cpp.hex:
avrdude: load data flash data from input file FPS_Enroll.cpp.hex:
```

```
avrdude: input file FPS_Enroll.cpp.hex auto detected as Intel Hex
avrdude: input file FPS_Enroll.cpp.hex contains 11458 bytes
avrdude: reading on-chip flash data:

Reading | ################################################## | 100% 2.21s

avrdude: verifying ...
avrdude: 11458 bytes of flash verified

avrdude: safemode: lfuse reads as 0
avrdude: safemode: hfuse reads as 0
avrdude: safemode: efuse reads as 0
avrdude: safemode: Fuses OK

avrdude done.  Thank you.
```

If there is a problem, first check to see whether the jumpers are attached and then try again.

This script will output to the serial port at 9600 baud, so we need to change /dev/tty04 to reflect this:

```
sudo stty -F /dev/tty04 9600
```

Finally, let's display the output of the serial port with:

```
cat /dev/tty04
```

The script is patiently waiting for you to enroll a finger. Place your finger on the reader and watch the output of the serial port and follow the instructions. A successful enrollment looks like this:

```
Remove finger
Press same finger again
Remove finger
Press same finger yet again
Remove finger
Enrolling Successful
```

If there is a problem, and the enrollment process can be a bit finicky, you'll need to reset the ATmega and re-attempt enrollment. In the same repository is a script, reset.sh, that simply toggles the ATmega reset line. If you have troubles, reset your ATmega and try again.

Uploading the biometric detection sketch

With the sensor now trained to recognize your fingerprint, we'll upload a sketch that will lock out the CryptoCape until you present your fingerprint. Specifically, it will prevent access to the chips on the CryptoCape from the BBB. We'll accomplish this by *jamming* the SCL line on the I2C bus.

One weakness of I2C is that one misaligned device can disrupt the entire bus. On the CryptoCape, every IC is connected to the same I2C bus. We'll exploit this for this project. The ATmega will hold the SCL low until a successful fingerprint is received. This essentially jams the bus since the master, the BBB, can't generate the start condition.

The software running on the BBB will hang until the ATmega releases the lock. Typically, this is a very undesirable effect. For this project, however, it illustrates how two microprocessors can interact and even interfere with one another. In the following screenshot, you can see the effect of this jamming of Salee Logic Analyzer software. Once the SCL is released, the BBB is finally able to send a start condition.

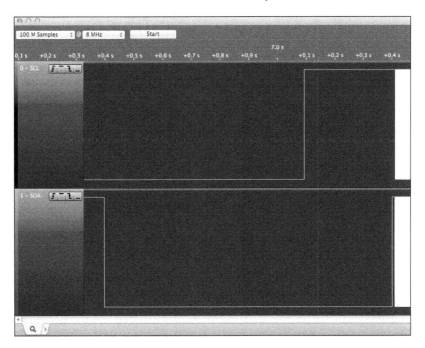

In the `FPS_CryptoCape.ino` file, this is accomplished by setting digital output 2 as an output and then pulling the line low. When a fingerprint is recognized, the pin is configured as an input, which prevents the ATmega from pulling the line either high or low and allows normal I2C operation.

Add a jumper wire from *D2* on the ATmega breakout pads to the *SCL* pad near the TPM on the CryptoCape. This is that one extra wire that will allow the ATmega to lock out the BBB's access to the I2C bus. Once you add that wire, upload the `FPS_CryptoCape.cpp.hex`, which you can either compile yourself or use the pre-compiled version. The wires on your CryptoCape should look like the following image:

Upload the sketch as before and then listen to the serial port with the same `cat /dev/tty04` command. You will see the ATmega waiting for the sensor's fingerprint. Present your fingerprint to the sensor and it will then print a verification when complete:

```
Please press finger

Verified ID:0
```

You will also notice that the green LED on the CryptoCape will turn off. While the LED is on, the ATmega is locking out your BBB from accessing the CryptoCape.

Security analysis of the biometric system

How secure is our biometric system? While it does prevent software on the BBB from using the CryptoCape until a valid fingerprint is accepted, the system is easily defeated by pulling (or cutting) the line from D2 to SCL. Without the electrical connection, the ATmega can't interfere with the I2C bus. However, depending on your installation, an attacker may have a difficult time physically accessing the hardware. The process of assessing vulnerabilities and mitigations to those vulnerabilities is known as **threat modeling**. In the previous chapter, the Tor design stated that it can't defend against a global passive adversary. In your implementation of our biometric system, maybe access to the jamming line is not a threat because you've placed your BBB in an adamantium box. There is no perfectly secure system so a threat model helps us understand the strengths, weaknesses, and assumptions of our system. We'll see more threat modeling in our final two chapters.

Summary

This chapter provided a close look at BeagleBone capes and the CryptoCape. We introduced the idea of trusted computing and built a biometric authentication system. We've shown the normal use case for I2C devices and illustrated how one rogue device can corrupt the entire bus.

In the next chapter, we'll use the BBB to protect e-mail encryption and signing keys for **Pretty Good Privacy** (**PGP**) and its free software implementation: GPG.

4
Protecting GPG Keys with a Trusted Platform Module

After our investigation into BBB hardware security, we'll now use that technology to protect your personal encryption keys for the popular GPG software. GPG is a free implementation of the OpenPGP standard. This standard was developed based on the work of Philip Zimmerman and his **Pretty Good Privacy** (**PGP**) software. PGP has a complex socio-political backstory, which we'll briefly cover before getting into the project. For the project, we'll treat the BBB as a separate cryptographic co-processor and use the CryptoCape, with a keypad code entry device, to protect our GPG keys when they are not in use.

Specifically, we will do the following:

- Tell you a little about the history and importance of the PGP software
- Perform basic threat modeling to analyze your project
- Create a strong PGP key using the free GPG software
- Teach you to use the TPM to protect encryption keys

History of PGP

The software used in this chapter would have once been considered a munition by the U.S. Government. Exporting it without a license from the government, would have violated the **International Traffic in Arms Regulations** (**ITAR**). As late as the early 1990s, cryptography was heavily controlled and restricted. While the early 90s are filled with numerous accounts by crypto-activists, all of which are well documented in Steven Levy's *Crypto*, there is one man in particular who was the driving force behind the software in this project: Philip Zimmerman.

Philip Zimmerman had a small pet project around the year 1990, which he called **Pretty Good Privacy**. Motivated by a strong childhood passion for codes and ciphers, combined with a sense of political activism against a government capable of strong electronic surveillance, he set out to create a strong encryption program for the people (Levy 2001).

One incident in particular helped to motivate Zimmerman to finish PGP and publish his work. This was the language that the then U.S. Senator Joseph Biden added to Senate Bill #266, which would mandate that:

> *"Providers of electronic communication services and manufacturers of electronic communications service equipment shall ensure that communication systems permit the government to obtain the plaintext contents of voice, data, and other communications when appropriately authorized by law."*

In 1991, in a rush to release PGP 1.0 before it was illegal, Zimmerman released his software as a freeware to the Internet. Subsequently, after PGP spread, the U.S. Government opened a criminal investigation on Zimmerman for the violation of the U.S. export laws. Zimmerman, in what is best described as a *legal hack*, published the entire source code of PGP, including instructions on how to scan it back into digital form, as a book. As Zimmerman describes:

> *"It would be politically difficult for the Government to prohibit the export of a book that anyone may find in a public library or a bookstore."*

> *(Zimmerman, 1995)*

A book published in the public domain would no longer fall under ITAR export controls. The genie was out of the bottle; the government dropped its case against Zimmerman in 1996.

Reflecting on the Crypto Wars

Zimmerman's battle is considered a resilient victory. Many other outspoken supporters of strong cryptography, known as **cypherpunks**, also won battles popularizing and spreading encryption technology. But if the Crypto Wars were won in the early nineties, why hasn't cryptography become ubiquitous? Well, to a degree, it has. When you make purchases online, it should be protected by strong cryptography. Almost nobody would insist that their bank or online store *not* use cryptography and most probably feel more secure that they do. But what about personal privacy protecting software? For these tools, habits must change as the normal e-mail, chat, and web browsing tools are insecure by default. This change causes tension and resistance towards adoption.

Also, security tools are notoriously hard to use. In the seminal paper on security usability, researchers conclude that the then PGP version 5.0, complete with a **Graphical User Interface (GUI)**, was not able to prevent users, who were inexperienced with cryptography but all of whom had at least some college education, from making catastrophic security errors (Whitten 1999). Glenn Greenwald delayed his initial contact with Edward Snowden for roughly two months because he thought GPG was *too complicated* to use (Greenwald, 2014). Snowden absolutely refused to share anything with Greenwald until he installed GPG.

GPG and PGP enable an individual to protect their own communications. Implicitly, you must also trust the receiving party not to forward your plaintext communication. GPG expects you to protect your private key and does not rely on a third party. While this adds some complexity and maintenance processes, trusting a third party with your private key can be disastrous. In August of 2013, Ladar Levison decided to shut down his own company, Lavabit, an e-mail provider, rather than turn over his users' data to the authorities. Levison courageously pulled the plug on his company rather then turn over the data.

The Lavabit service generated and stored your private key. While this key was encrypted to the user's password, it still enabled the server to have access to the raw key. Even though the Lavabit service alleviated users from managing their private key themselves, it enabled the awkward position for Levison. To use GPG properly, you should never turn over your private key. For a complete analysis of Lavabit, see Moxie Marlinspike's blog post at `http://www.thoughtcrime.org/blog/lavabit-critique/`.

Given the breadth and depth of state surveillance capabilities, there is a re-kindled interest in protecting one's privacy. Researchers are now designing secure protocols, with these threats in mind (Borisov, 2014). Philip Zimmerman ended the chapter on *Why Do You Need PGP?* in the *Official PGP User's Guide* with the following statement, which is as true today as it was when first inked:

> *"PGP empowers people to take their privacy into their own hands. There's a growing social need for it."*

Developing a threat model

At the end of the previous chapter, we introduced the concept of a threat model. A **threat model** is an analysis of the security of the system that identifies assets, threats, vulnerabilities, and risks. Like any model, the depth of the analysis can vary. In the upcoming section, we'll present a cursory analysis so that you can start thinking about this process. This analysis will also help us understand the capabilities and limitations of our project.

Outlining the key protection system

The first step of our analysis is to clearly provide a description of the system we are trying to protect. In this project, we'll build a logical GPG co-processor using the BBB and the CryptoCape. We'll store the GPG keys on the BBB and then connect to the BBB over **Secure Shell (SSH)** to use the keys and to run GPG. The CryptoCape will be used to encrypt your GPG key when not in use, known as **at rest**. We'll add a keypad to collect a numeric code, which will be provided to the TPM. This will allow the TPM to unwrap your GPG key.

The idea for this project was inspired by Peter Gutmann's work on open source cryptographic co-processors (Gutmann, 2000). The BBB, when acting as a co-processor to a host, is extremely flexible, and considering the power usage, relatively high in performance. By running sensitive code that will have access to cleartext encryption keys on a separate hardware, we gain an extra layer of protection (or at the minimum, a layer of indirection).

Identifying the assets we need to protect

Before we can protect anything, we must know what to protect. The most important assets are the GPG private keys. With these keys, an attacker can decrypt past encrypted messages, recover future messages, and use the keys to impersonate you. By protecting your private key, we are also protecting your reputation, which is another asset. Our decrypted messages are also an asset. An attacker may not care about your key if he/she can easily access your decrypted messages. The BBB itself is an asset that needs protecting. If the BBB is rendered inoperable, then an attacker has successfully prevented you from accessing your private keys, which is known as a **Denial-Of-Service (DOS)**.

Threat identification

To identify the threats against our system, we need to classify the capabilities of our adversaries. This is a highly personal analysis, but we can generalize our adversaries into three archetypes: a well funded state actor, a skilled cracker, and a jealous ex-lover. The state actor has nearly limitless resources both from a financial and personnel point of view. The cracker is a skilled operator, but lacks the funding and resources of the state actor. The jealous ex-lover is not a sophisticated computer attacker, but is very motivated to do you harm.

Unfortunately, if you are the target of directed surveillance from a state actor, you probably have much bigger problems than your GPG keys. This actor can put your entire life under monitoring and why go through the trouble of stealing your GPG keys when the hidden video camera in the wall records everything on your screen.

Also, it's reasonable to assume that everyone you are communicating with is also under surveillance and it only takes one mistake from one person to reveal your plans for world domination.

 The adage by Benjamin Franklin is apropos here: *Three may keep a secret if two of them are dead.*

However, properly using GPG will protect you from global passive surveillance. When used correctly, neither your Internet Service Provider, nor your e-mail provider, or any passive attacker would learn the contents of your messages. The passive adversary is not going to engage your system, but they could monitor a significant amount of Internet traffic in an attempt to *collect it all*. Therefore, the confidentiality of your message should remain protected.

We'll assume the cracker trying to harm you is remote and does not have physical access to your BBB. We'll also assume the worst case that the cracker has compromised your host machine. In this scenario there is, unfortunately, a lot that the cracker can perform. He can install a key logger and capture everything, including the password that is typed on your computer. He will not be able to get the code that we'll enter on the BBB; however, he would be able to log in to the BBB when the key is available.

The jealous ex-lover doesn't understand computers very well, but he doesn't need to, because he knows how to use a golf club. He knows that this BBB connected to your computer is somehow important to you because you've talked his ear off about this really cool project that you read in a book. He physically can destroy the BBB and with it, your private key (and probably the relationship as well!).

Identifying the risks

How likely are the previous risks? The risk of active government surveillance in most countries is fortunately low. However, the consequences of this attack are very damaging. The risk of being caught up in passive surveillance by a state actor, as we have learned from Edward Snowden, is very likely. However, by using GPG, we add protection against this threat. An active cracker seeking you harm is probably unlikely. Contracting keystroke-capturing malware, however, is probably not an unreasonable event. A 2013 study by Microsoft concluded that 8 out of every 1,000 computers were infected with malware. You may be tempted to play these odds but let's rephrase this statement: in a group of 125 computers, one is infected with malware. A school or university easily has more computers than this. Lastly, only you can assess the risk of a jealous ex-lover.

For the full Microsoft report, refer to `http://blogs.technet.com/b/security/archive/2014/03/31/united-states-malware-infection-rate-more-than-doubles-in-the-first-half-of-2013.aspx`.

Mitigating the identified risks

If you find yourself the target of a state, this project alone is not going to help much. We can protect ourselves somewhat from the cracker with two strategies. The first is instead of connecting the BBB to your laptop or computer, you can use the BBB as a standalone machine and transfer files via a microSD card. This is known as an **air-gap**. With a dedicated monitor and keyboard, it is much less likely for software vulnerabilities to break the gap and infect the BBB. However, this comes as a high level of personal inconvenience, depending on how often you encrypt files. If you consider the risk of running the BBB attached to your computer too high, create an air-gapped BBB for maximum protection. If you deem the risk low, because you've hardened your computer and have other protection mechanism, then keep the BBB attached to the computer.

An air-gapped computer can still be compromised. In 2010, a highly specialized worm known as Stuxnet was able to spread to networked isolated machines through USB flash drives.

The second strategy is to somehow enter the GPG passphrase directly into the BBB without using the host's keyboard. After we complete the project, we'll suggest a mechanism to do this, but it is slightly more complicated. This would eliminate the threat of the key logger since the pin is directly entered.

The mitigation against the ex-lover is to treat your BBB as you would your own wallet, and don't leave it out of your sight. It's slightly larger than you would want, but it's certainly small enough to fit in a small backpack or briefcase.

Summarizing our threat model

Our threat model, while cursory, illustrates the thought process one should go through before using or developing security technologies. The term threat model is specific to the security industry, but it's really just proper planning. The purpose of this analysis is to find *logic bugs* and prevent you from spending thousands of dollars on high-tech locks for your front door when you keep your backdoor unlocked. Now that we understand what we are trying to protect and why it is important to use GPG, let's build the project.

Generating GPG keys

First, we need to install GPG on the BBB. It is mostly likely already installed, but you can check and install it with the following command:

```
sudo apt-get install gnupg gnupg-curl
```

Next, we need to add a secret key. For those that already have a secret key, you can import your secret key ring, `secring.gpg`, to your `~/.gnupg` folder. For those that want to create a new key, on the BBB, proceed to the upcoming section.

 This project assumes some familiarity with GPG. If GPG is new to you, the Free Software Foundation maintains the **Email Self-Defense** guide which is a very approachable introduction to the software and can be found at `https://emailselfdefense.fsf.org/en/index.html`.

Generating entropy

If you decided to create a new key on the BBB, there are a few technicalities we must consider. First of all, GPG will need a lot of random data to generate the keys. The amount of random data available in the kernel is proportional to the amount of entropy that is available. You can check the available entropy with the following command:

```
cat /proc/sys/kernel/random/entropy_avail
```

If this command returns a relatively low number, under 200, then GPG will not have enough entropy to generate a key. On a PC, one can increase the amount of entropy by interacting with the computer such as typing on the keyboard or moving the mouse. However, such sources of entropy are difficult for embedded systems, and in our current setup, we don't have the luxury of moving a mouse.

Fortunately, there are a few tools to help us. If your BBB is running kernel version 3.13 or later, we can use the hardware random number generator on the AM3358 to help us out. You'll need to install the `rng-tools` package. Once installed, you can edit `/etc/default/rng-tools` and add the following line to register the hardware random number generated for `rng-tools`:

```
HRNGDEVICE=/dev/hwrng
```

After this, you should start the `rng-tools` daemon with:

```
/etc/init.d/rng-tools start
```

If you don't have /dev/hwrng—and currently, the chips on the CryptoCape do not yet have character device support and aren't available to /dev/hwrng—then you can install haveged. This daemon implements the **Hardware Volatile Entropy Gathering and Expansion (HAVEGE)** algorithm, the details of which are available at http://www.irisa.fr/caps/projects/hipsor/. This daemon will ensure that the BBB maintains a pool of entropy, which will be sufficient for generating a GPG key on the BBB.

Creating a good gpg.conf file

Before you generate your key, we need to establish some more secure defaults for GPG. As we discussed earlier, it is still not as easy as it should be to use e-mail encryption. Riseup.net, an e-mail provider with a strong social cause, maintains an OpenPGP best practices guide at https://help.riseup.net/en/security/ message-security/openpgp/best-practices. This guide details how to harden your GPG configuration and provides the motivation behind each option. It is well worth a read to understand the intricacies of GPG key management.

Jacob Applebaum maintains an implementation of these best practices, which you should download from https://github.com/ioerror/duraconf/raw/ master/configs/gnupg/gpg.conf and save as your ~/.gnupg/gpg.conf file. The configuration is well commented and you can refer to the best practices guide available at Riseup.net for more information. There are three entries, however, that you should modify. The first is default-key, which is the fingerprint of your primary GPG key. Later in this chapter, we'll show you how to retrieve that fingerprint. We can't perform this action now because we don't have a key yet. The second is keyserver-options ca-cert-file, which is the certificate authority for the **keyserver pool**. Keyservers host your public keys and a keyserver pool is a redundant collection of keyservers. The instructions on Riseup.net gives the details on how to download and install that certificate. Lastly, you can use Tor to fetch updates on your keys.

The act of you requesting a public key from a keyserver signals that you have a potential interest in communicating with the owner of that key. This metadata might be more interesting to a passive adversary than the contents of your message, since it reveals your social network. As we learned in *Chapter 2, Circumventing Censorship with a Tor Bridge*, Tor is apt at protecting traffic analysis. You probably don't want to store your GPG keys on the same BBB as your bridge, so a second BBB would help here. On your GPG BBB, you need to only run Tor as a client, which is its default configuration. Then you can update keyserver-options http-proxy to point to your Tor SOCKS proxy running on localhost.

The **Electronic Frontier Foundation** (**EFF**) provides some hypothetical examples on the telling nature of metadata, for example, *They (the government) know you called the suicide prevention hotline from the Golden Gate Bridge. But the topic of the call remains a secret.* Refer to the EFF blog post at `https://www.eff.org/deeplinks/2013/06/why-metadata-matters` for more details.

Generating the key

Now you can generate your GPG key. Follow the on screen instructions and don't include a comment. Depending on your entropy source, this could take a while. This example took 10 minutes using `haveged` as the entropy collector. There are various opinions on what to set as the expiration date. If this is your first GPG, try one year at first. You can always make a new key or extend the same one. If you set the key to never expire and you lose the key, by forgetting the passphrase, people will still think it's valid unless you revoke it. Also, be sure to set the user ID to a name that matches some sort of identification, which will make it easier for people to verify that the holder of the private key is the same person as a certified piece of paper. The command to create a new key is `gpg --gen-key`:

```
Please select what kind of key you want:
    (1) RSA and RSA (default)
    (2) DSA and Elgamal
    (3) DSA (sign only)
    (4) RSA (sign only)
Your selection? 1
RSA keys may be between 1024 and 4096 bits long.
What keysize do you want? (2048) 4096
Requested keysize is 4096 bits
Please specify how long the key should be valid.
        0 = key does not expire
    <n>  = key expires in n days
    <n>w = key expires in n weeks
    <n>m = key expires in n months
    <n>y = key expires in n years
Key is valid for? (0) 1y
Key expires at Sat 06 Jun 2015 10:07:07 PM UTC
Is this correct? (y/N) y

You need a user ID to identify your key; the software constructs the user
ID
```

```
from the Real Name, Comment and Email Address in this form:
    "Heinrich Heine (Der Dichter) <heinrichh@duesseldorf.de>"

Real name: Tyrone Slothrop
Email address: tyrone.slothrop@yoyodyne.com
Comment:
You selected this USER-ID:
    "Tyrone Slothrop <tyrone.slothrop@yoyodyne.com>"

Change (N)ame, (C)omment, (E)mail or (O)kay/(Q)uit? O
You need a Passphrase to protect your secret key.

We need to generate a lot of random bytes. It is a good idea to perform
some other action (type on the keyboard, move the mouse, utilize the
disks) during the prime generation; this gives the random number
generator a better chance to gain enough entropy.
......+++++
..+++++

gpg: key 0xABD9088171345468 marked as ultimately trusted
public and secret key created and signed.

gpg: checking the trustdb
gpg: 3 marginal(s) needed, 1 complete(s) needed, PGP trust model
gpg: depth: 0  valid:   1  signed:   0  trust: 0-, 0q, 0n, 0m, 0f, 1u
gpg: next trustdb check due at 2015-06-06
pub   4096R/0xABD9088171345468 2014-06-06 [expires: 2015-06-06]
      Key fingerprint = CBF9 1404 7214 55C5 C477  B688 ABD9 0881 7134
5468
uid                   [ultimate] Tyrone Slothrop <tyrone.slothrop@yoyodyne.
com>
sub   4096R/0x9DB8B6ACC7949DD1 2014-06-06 [expires: 2015-06-06]

gpg --gen-key  320.62s user 0.32s system 51% cpu 10:23.26 total
```

From this example, we know that our secret key is 0xABD9088171345468. If you end
up creating multiple keys, but use just one of them more regularly, you can edit your
gpg.conf file and add the following line:

```
default-key 0xABD9088171345468
```

Postgeneration maintenance

In order for people to send you encrypted messages, they need to know your public key. Having your public key server can help distribute your public key. You can post your key as follows, and replace the fingerprint with your primary key ID:

```
gpg --send-keys 0xABD9088171345468
```

 GPG does not rely on third parties and expects you to perform key management. To ease this burden, the OpenPGP standards define the Web-of-Trust as a mechanism to verify other users' keys. Details on how to participate in the Web-of-Trust can be found in the GPG Privacy Handbook at https://www.gnupg.org/gph/en/manual/x334.html.

You are also going to want to create a revocation certificate. A revocation certificate is needed when you want to revoke your key. You would do this when the key has been compromised, say if it was stolen. Or more likely, if the BBB fails and you can no longer access your key. Generate the certificate and follow the ensuing prompts replacing the ID with your key ID:

```
gpg --output revocation-certificate.asc --gen-revoke 0xABD9088171345468
```

```
sec   4096R/0xABD9088171345468 2014-06-06 Tyrone Slothrop <tyrone.
slothrop@yoyodyne.com>


Create a revocation certificate for this key? (y/N) y
Please select the reason for the revocation:
  0 = No reason specified
  1 = Key has been compromised
  2 = Key is superseded
  3 = Key is no longer used
  Q = Cancel
(Probably you want to select 1 here)
Your decision? 0
Enter an optional description; end it with an empty line:
>
Reason for revocation: No reason specified
(No description given)
Is this okay? (y/N) y


You need a passphrase to unlock the secret key for
```

```
user: "Tyrone Slothrop <tyrone.slothrop@yoyodyne.com>"
4096-bit RSA key, ID 0xABD9088171345468, created 2014-06-06


ASCII armored output forced.
Revocation certificate created.


Please move it to a medium which you can hide away; if Mallory gets
access to this certificate he can use it to make your key unusable.
It is smart to print this certificate and store it away, just in case
your media become unreadable.  But have some caution:  The print system
of your machine might store the data and make it available to others!
```

Do take the advice and move this file off the BeagleBone. Printing it out and storing it somewhere safe is a good option, or burn it to a CD.

The lifespan of a CD or DVD may not be as long as you think. The United States National Archives Frequently Asked Questions (FAQ) page on optical storage media states that:

"CD/DVD experiential life expectancy is 2 to 5 years even though published life expectancies are often cited as 10 years, 25 years, or longer."

Refer to their website http://www.archives.gov/records-mgmt/initiatives/temp-opmedia-faq.html for more details.

Lastly, create an encrypted backup of your encryption key and consider storing that in a safe location on durable media.

Using GPG

With your GPG private key created or imported, you can now use GPG on the BBB as you would on any other computer. In *Chapter 1, Creating Your BeagleBone Black Development Environment*, you installed Emacs on your host computer. If you follow the GNU/Linux instructions, you can also install Emacs on the BBB. If you do, you'll enjoy automatic GPG encryption and decryption for files that end in the .gpg extension. For example, suppose you want to send a message to your good friend, Pirate Prentice, whose GPG key you already have. Compose your message in Emacs, and then save it with a .gpg extension. Emacs will prompt you to select the public keys for encryption and will automatically encrypt the buffer. If a GPG-encrypted message is encrypted to a public key, with which you have the corresponding private key, Emacs will automatically decrypt the message if it ends with .gpg. When using Emacs from the terminal, the prompt for encryption should look like the following screenshot:

```
1Josh,
2
3We've found rocket 00000.
4
5T.S.




-UUU:**--F1  rocket.gpg     All of 39   (5,4)      [(Text ws Projectile Pre Abbrev
1Select recipients for encryption.
2If no one is selected, symmetric encryption will be performed.
3- `m' to mark a key on the line
4- `u' to unmark a key on the line
5[Cancel][OK]
6
7  -  7BFA5031BD2EDEA6 Joshua Brian Datko <jbd@cryptotronix.com>
8  u ABD9088171345468 Tyrone Slothrop <tyrone.slothrop@yoyodyne.com>


-UUU:%*--F1  *Keys*         All of 310  (1,0)      [(Keys Projectile Pre)] --------
```

Protecting your GPG key with a TPM

If you want, you could stop the project now and happily use GPG on your BBB. But if you do, you would miss out on adding some extra protection with the CryptoCape, specifically, the **Trusted Platform Module (TPM)**. In the upcoming sections, we will use the TPM to protect our GPG private key.

Introducing trusted computing

The TPM is a cryptographic co-processor. The TPM on the CryptoCape is Atmel's embedded I2C version, which conforms to version 1.2 of the TPM spec published by the **Trusted Computing Group (TCG)**. The TCG is an industry consortium that maintains and develops open specifications for trusted computing. *Trusted* in this sense is the definition from RFC 4949: *a system that operates as expected, according to design and policy.*

Cryptographically, TPM 1.2 is limited. It implements the RSA algorithm, SHA-1, has an internal random number generator, and some limited storage. It does not provide any symmetric ciphers. These limitations were a result of the design goal for a low cost embeddable module. Symmetric ciphers were eliminated, because with the TPM, one can protect the symmetric keys at rest and allow the much more powerful host computer to operate on them.

The TPM 1.2 specification is, in total, over 700 pages. We will focus on a unique feature of the TPM that enables many of its security features: **Platform Control Registers (PCRs)**. PCRs are TPM registers that can always be read but may only be written to with the **extend operation**. The extend operation takes the current value of the 20 byte PCR, combines it with a 20 byte input value, and sets the new PCR value to the SHA-1 result of the combination. The key point is that once a PCR is set, it can't be reversed. It can only be continhued to be combined in future extend operations.

At first, it may not be obvious how this feature helps. Let's consider an example. On boot, your computer's BIOS, prior to loading the bootloader, first sends a SHA-1 hash of the bootloader to the TPM to extend one of the PCRs. It then loads the bootloader. The bootloader performs the same operation on your kernel. The kernel then performs the same operation on various startup systems before finally allowing normal user operation. At the end of this process, the PCRs will be populated with a series of hash values.

The values of these registers represent a trusted measurement of your system. Now, say malware has infected your computer and has modified the boot process. On next boot, at least one of the PCRs will have a drastically different value than previously recorded. PCRs enable measurements of the boot process which provide assertions of the boot process.

There are several terms relating to the TPM-protected boot process. Secure boot will halt the boot processes if the PCR values do not match a known configuration. Authenticated boot simply measures the boot process and allows remote parties to make assertions on the pedigree of the boot process. Trusted boot refers to a system that uses both authenticated and secure boots.

Encrypting data to a PCR state

The TPM supports another feature that builds on the state of the PCRs. As previously mentioned, the TPM can perform RSA encryption. However, the TPM can also combine the state of the PCRs to the encryption in a process known as **sealing**. Once data is sealed to a PCR value, it can only be decrypted when the PCR matches the same value as when the encryption was performed.

How is this going to help us protect our GPG key? We will encrypt the GPG key to a known PCR state. We'll use the numeric code entered from the keypad connected to the CryptoCape as input into this PCR state. When the TPM decrypts the GPG private key, it will be available for use by GPG as usual. While GPG private keys are already protected with a passphrase, the TPM provides extra protection for the key at rest. The passphrase could still be captured with a keylogger, but our key won't be available until the BBB boots with the CryptoCape attached and the code entered directly into the BBB.

This system also helps in preventing offline attacks on the numeric code. The PCR value, once extended with the correct code, will allow unsealing of the data. But, if the wrong code is entered, the PCR value will be incorrect and the only way to reset the PCR, if that PCR is one of the *non-resettable* PCRs, is to reboot.

Adding the keypad

We're going to need a way to enter this code into the BBB. This code is used to populate one of the TPM's PCRs that will be used to seal the GPG key. This keypad will be connected to the ATmega328p on the CryptoCape. While the BBB is more than capable of handling the I/O for the keypad, by using the ATmega328p, we take advantage of code reuse. For most hardware products in the SparkFun catalog, there exists at least an unofficial Arduino library. If the components aren't available at SparkFun, then you should be able to find similar parts from the product descriptions. In the case of the keypad, there is an official library. The hardware for this project is listed in the following table:

Device	SparkFun number
CryptoCape	DEV-12773
Keypad	COM-08653
F/F jumper wires	PRT-08430
Male breakaway headers	PRT-00116

To build this Arduino library, you'll first need to install the `Keypad` library from the Arduino playground site: `http://playground.arduino.cc/code/Keypad`. Then clone the following repository from GitHub:

```
git clone https://github.com/jbdatko/beagle-bone-for-secret-agents.git
```

In the `ch4` code folder, you'll find both the `keypad.ino` source and the compiled hex that is ready to be loaded onto the 328p. From *Chapter 3*, *Adding Hardware Security with the CryptoCape*, remember that compiled sketches can be uploaded to the ATmega328p with the following command, just be sure to install the program jumpers:

```
sudo ./upload.sh keypad_cryptocape.cpp.hex
```

This program has the 328p joining the I2C bus at hex address 0x42. It then waits to receive data from an I2C master device, the BBB, and then will collect your five-digit code from the keypad. You have ten seconds to enter a five-digit code and the timer starts once the CryptoCape LED is lit. Each time you press a key, the LED will momentarily flash. Once all five characters are collected, the LED will turn off.

To connect the keypad to the CryptoCape, you first need to solder 0.1" male pins to the keypad. Also, you'll need to solder the 0.1" male header pins to the CryptoCape ATmega328p pads. Once the pins are installed, now you need to connect a jumper wire from the keypad to the CryptoCape. Note that the keypad has nine pins but only seven are used. Consider the first pin, closest to the * character as *pin 0*. Connect the jumpers per the following table:

Keypad pin	Arduino digital pin
3	D2
1	D3
5	D4
2	D5
7	D6
6	D7
4	D8

The keypad, when attached to the CryptoCape, should look like the following image:

The case shown in the image is logic supply's plated steel chassis. It is available on their website: http://www.logicsupply.com/components/beaglebone/boards-cases-kits/bb100-orange/.

Now, we need some software that will initiate the code collection process on the ATmega328p. Remember that the software needs to collect the code and then extend the PCR. In the previously listed repository is a file, keypad.c, which does exactly this. To build this program, you'll need the development package of the open source TCG software stack:

```
sudo apt-get install libtspi-dev
```

Then you should be able to compile the program with:

```
gcc keypad.c -o getgpgpin -ltspi
```

Taking ownership of the TPM

Before we use the TPM, we must first take ownership of it. Taking ownership establishes an owner password for maintenance operations and a password for one of the root keys inside the TPM, the **Storage Root Key** (**SRK**) (pronounced *shark*). You can set the administrator password to any password you want, but to work with legacy software, you'll want to set the SRK to the *well-known password* of twenty zeros. You can set a unique SRK password if you want, but the TrouSerS software, the software used to control the TPM, includes a command-line parameter to set the password to its well-known value for a reason. First install tpm-tools:

```
sudo apt-get install tpm-tools
```

Then you should restart your BBB with the CryptoCape attached. This will ensure that the TPM kernel driver and associate software load correctly. To check if everything is working properly issue the following command:

```
dmesg | grep TPM
```

This should return:

```
[    5.370109] tpm_i2c_atmel 1-0029: Issuing TPM_STARTUP
```

Then check for the daemon by issuing:

```
ps aux | grep tcsd
```

This command should return something like this:

```
tss   799  0.0  0.1  11492   980 ?  Ss Jun08 0:00 /usr/sbin/tcsd
```

Then you can take ownership of the TPM as follows:

```
tpm_takeownership -z -l debug
```

You'll be prompted to enter an owner password. The -z option sets the SRK to the well-known passphrase. The response should be:

```
Tspi_Context_Create success
Enter owner password:
Confirm password:
Tspi_Context_Connect success
Tspi_Context_GetTpmObject success
Tspi_GetPolicyObject success
Tspi_Policy_SetSecret success
Tspi_Context_CreateObject success
Tspi_GetPolicyObject success
Tspi_Policy_SetSecret success
Tspi_TPM_TakeOwnership success
tpm_takeownership succeeded
Tspi_Context_CloseObject success
Tspi_Context_FreeMemory success
Tspi_Context_Close success
```

Now you are ready to use the TPM.

 If you have the CryptoCape v02, then you will need to perform some additional steps. The version number is found on the bottom layer of the board, above the P8 header, near the open source hardware logo, which looks like a gear. The TPMs on this revision are shipped in compliance mode, which means the keys loaded on them are test keys. This helps test the TPM during manufacture, but the keys need to be changed by the end user. Refer to the page http://cryptotronix. com/cryptocape-tpm/ for more details.

Extending a PCR

We'll need to extend a PCR so that we can encrypt our GPG key. We'll arbitrarily choose PCR number 9. First let's view the PCR status to be sure that it is blank:

```
cat /sys/class/misc/tpm0/device/pcrs | grep PCR-09
```

This should return the current state of the PCR, which without using secure boot is:

`PCR-09:00 00 00 00 00 00 00 00 00 00 00 00 00 00 00 00 00 00 00 00`

Now, run the `getgpgpin` program from the following section. You should see the LED turn green on the CryptoCape and you have 10 seconds to enter a five-digit pin. Each time you press a key, the LED should briefly flash and when five digits have been entered, the LED will turn off. After 10 seconds, the `getgpgpin` program will silently exit. If you compiled the program with `#define DEBUG` set to `1`, you should see something like this:

```
54321
(Line 53, extend_pcr)  Create a Context
 returned 0x00000000. Success.
(Line 55, extend_pcr)  Connect to TPM
 returned 0x00000000. Success.
(Line 59, extend_pcr)  GetTPM Handle
 returned 0x00000000. Success.
(Line 62, extend_pcr)  Owner Policy
 returned 0x00000000. Success.
36987(Line 73, extend_pcr)  extend
 returned 0x00000000. Success.
```

Now, check your PCR status again:

`cat /sys/class/misc/tpm0/device/pcrs | grep PCR-09`

You should now have a populated PCR9:

`PCR-09:2B 1E 41 10 EB A0 91 9E B4 89 0E 04 83 0B 70 C5 C2 AA 23 44`

You can only enter the code once. If you try it again, the program will extend PCR9 again using the now incorrect PCR state as input into the next. Now, let's seal our GPG secret key ring:

`tpm_sealdata -p 9 -i secring.gpg -o secring.gpg.tpm -z -l debug`

You can remove `-l debug` if you wish and the command will silently complete. Let's test decryption:

`tpm_unsealdata -i secring.gpg.tpm -o deleteme -z`

It should silently complete on success. You can now delete the temporary file `deleteme` and the original `secring.gpg`. You did make an encrypted backup, right? You'll probably want to delete the file in a more secure fashion. The secure remove tool `srm` does just that and overwrites the file numerous times before deleting. To install use the following command:

```
sudo apt-get install secure-delete
```

Then use just as you would `rm`.

Bunnie Huang and Sean Cross (also known as *xobs*) presented a talk at the **30th Chaos Communication Congress (30C3)** on hacking SD cards. Your SD or eMMC includes a small microcontroller that manages the attached flash memory. This microcontroller is perfectly situated to act as a Man-in-the-Middle attacker and manipulate the data you store on the device. For example, the microcontroller could keep a backup copy of your data since it would report to your computer a storage capacity of 8GB, but actually it contains a 16 GB flash chip. More information can be found on Bunnie's blog at `http://www.bunniestudios.com/blog/?p=3554`.

Unlocking your key at startup

Finally, we need to automate this process. When the BBB boots, we want it to collect the code, extend the PCR, and unwrap the GPG keys so that they are ready to use. We'll make an `init.d` script that will handle this, but we still need to deal with the GPG key. We don't want an unwrapped GPG key lying around the disk, even if it is protected with a password. Instead, we'll keep the GPG keys on a `ramfs`, which will never touch persistent storage.

To create the `ramfs`, add the following to `/etc/fstab`:

```
ramfs    /mnt/ramdisk ramfs nodev,nosuid,noexec,nodiratime,size=1M,uid=10
00,gid=1002    0 0
```

Be sure to replace your uid and gid with the appropriate values for your user. This can be obtained by running the `id` command. Either reboot or run `mount -a` to reload the `fstab`. Since GPG expects the `secring.gpg` to live in `~/.gnupg/secring.gpg`, we'll create a link from there to the ramdisk. Create the following symlink:

```
ln -s /mnt/ramdisk/secring.gpg ~/.gnupg/secring.gpg
```

Now, we want a script to run on boot. In the `beagle-bone-for-secret-agents/` `ch4` repository, there is a script, `tpm_gpg`, which you can copy to `/etc/init.d/`. This script expects `getgpgpin` to live in `/usr/local/bin` and that your `secring.gpg` is in the normal place. Edit as desired. To register this script, run as root:

`update-rc.d tpm_gpg defaults`

With the script in place, the ramdisk set to mount at boot, the ATmega programmed to collect the code, and the hardware attached, reboot one more time. Watch for the CryptoCape LED to turn on, enter your pin, and then log back in to the BBB. If your GPG key is in `/mnt/ramdisk`, congratulations, you have just used your TPM to protect your GPG key! Because of the symlink, all GPG-related programs will use the keys just as usual. If not, recompile `keypad.c` with debug set to `1` to make sure everything is working.

 While the ramfs is meant to ensure that the GPG key, which is still protected by a password, is destroyed without power, researchers have recovered keys from RAM in the past. Refer to the URL `https://` `citp.princeton.edu/research/memory/` on cold boot attacks.

Iterating on the threat model

Threat modeling and system design is an iterative process. The system we built in this chapter is a good start, but it can be improved. We identified a problem at the beginning of the chapter in that we still had to enter the GPG passphrase from a potentially compromised computer. The code entry on the keypad is currently only protecting the GPG key when the BBB is powered off. It also protects the key if an attacker who doesn't know the code boots the BBB, since the PCR will not have the correct value after the 10-second window has passed. To mitigate against the key logger attack, we would want to enter a passphrase directly into the BBB.

There is a piece of software called **gpg-agent**, which manages your passphrase per login session. It can support different types of *pin entry* programs. For example, one pin entry program is X-Windows-based and another supports a command-line interface. You could certainly create your own pin entry program that supported your custom hardware. However, when you create this custom pin entry, you'd want to consider the effect of a potentially weaker passphrase, one composed of only numbers, for your GPG key. This demonstrates the importance of re-evaluating your threat model as new features are added to the design to ensure the correctness of the original assumptions.

Also, you might want to consider adding an enclosure for your project. Your local hackerspace will be able to help you make a professionally looking enclosure. If you want something on the cheap, find a small translucent container and cut out room for the keypad and the connectors as shown in the following image:

Summary

In this chapter, you learned how GPG can protect e-mail confidentiality. We created a threat model for our system and showed how this analysis can help us understand the capabilities and limitations of our design. At the end, we successfully built a BBB GPG co-processor that uses a TPM to help protect the GPG keys at rest and got more practice combining a microcontroller with an embedded Linux platform.

In the next chapter, we will investigate another major privacy enhancing technology that is used to protect real-time chat. You'll learn about the unique cryptographic properties of **Off-the-Record (OTR)** and how to use OTR over an Internet Relay Chat gateway that is hosted by your BBB.

5
Chatting Off-the-Record

In this final chapter, we will use the **BeagleBone Black** (**BBB**) to protect the last bastion of your online life: real-time chats. With your e-mail protected by GPG and your browsing protected by Tor, we'll use the software called **Off-the-Record** (**OTR**) to protect instant messaging chats. OTR addresses a weakness in the PGP threat model and we will give an overview of the OTR design objectives before building the project. We'll also consolidate all of your chat networks to be managed over an Internet Relay Chat interface, which will run on your BBB. While this project doesn't require any additional hardware other than the BBB, the cryptographic concepts and networking interactions are slightly more challenging than the previous chapters. At the end of this chapter and the book, you will have had exposure to and become familiar with the three most effective tools to protect your privacy online.

In this chapter, you will do the following:

- Learn the difference between the cryptographic design between PGP and OTR
- Run an IRC to chat gateway with BitlBee
- Incorporate your IRC networks with the IRC bouncer ZNC
- Set up and use OTR chat on BitlBee and ZNC

Communicating Off-the-Record – a background

Before we investigate OTR, let's consider how we could encrypt our chat sessions. We could use GPG for chat. We'd have to know the public key of our correspondent, and each time we'd enter a message, it would encrypt and/or sign the message and send it along. Some chat networks don't have an equivalent e-mail address, so it could be awkward finding and verifying public keys. However, you can certainly imagine a chat system that worked this way; it's a slightly more synchronous version of GPG with e-mail.

Even if those technical problems are addressed there is a bigger issue lurking in PGP's design. Let's return to our friends Alice and Bob. Alice and Bob have been communicating with GPG for quite some time now. They use GPG flawlessly and religiously practice the best security hygiene. Until one day, when somebody gets a hold of Bob's private key. Now, there are several ways this could happen. Despite Bob's willpower, perhaps he just couldn't resist clicking on the *Watch cuTe kittys [sic]* link and malware infected his computer. Perhaps somebody stole his custom made GPG key hardware token and guessed his GPG passphrase. Regardless of how his private key was leaked, what matters is that now somebody else has it.

Bob, vigilant GPG user that he is, immediately revokes his key, which informs the world that the key is compromised. This warns others not to use that particular key and for future conversations, they should use a new key. But let's not forget about Alice and the many communiqués she exchanged with Bob. What's to make of Alice? This attacker, who has Bob's private key, can decrypt the entire past communication between Alice and Bob. All of it. All of a sudden, their conversation doesn't seem so private as Ian Goldberg, the designer of OTR, remarks about privacy in GPG communications.

Introducing Off-the-Record communication

While GPG has its place, if you are concerned about losing control of your private key, then maybe you should consider other tools. One tool, which was designed with this threat in mind, is called **Off-the-Record (OTR)** which was originally published in the paper *Off-the-Record Communication, or, Why Not To Use PGP* (Borisov 2004). OTR includes some cryptographic features and design goals that differ from PGP. For example, OTR was designed to incorporate *perfect forward secrecy*, which ensures that **session keys**, the keys that are encrypting the communication traffic, can't be re-derived if the longer term identity key is compromised. Also OTR only uses digital signatures for the initial authentication step; individual messages are not signed.

The session keys are derived independently by both parties through a **Diffie-Hellman Key-Exchange** protocol. The Diffie-Hellman protocol helps to solve a key distribution problem. Alice and Bob want to secure their communications with a symmetric cipher, but they both need the same key. Using Diffie-Hellman, they can both derive the shared key value over an insecure channel, without exposing the value of the key to a third party. OTR uses asymmetric cryptography in a Diffie-Hellman key-exchange, so that both parties can derive a shared AES key in counter-mode. **AES in counter-mode (AES-CTR)** uses AES as a stream cipher, the significance of which is discussed later in this section.

A simplified, two-minute description of the Diffie-Hellman Key Exchange is available at Khan Academy website `https://www.khanacademy.org/computing/computer-science/cryptography/modern-crypt/v/diffie-hellman-key-exchange--part-2`.

Another feature of OTR that is different than PGP is that OTR was designed with repudiability for messages, which is the ability to deny authorship or validity. PGP was designed for non-repudiation, which provides a proof, via your digital signature, that you indeed created that message. However, with OTR, neither Alice nor Bob can prove the other, or themselves, created a particular message. The details of this feature are a bit technical, but we'll provide a high-level summary since it is a clever use of **Message Authentication Codes (MACs)**.

A MAC is a small tag that accompanies a block of data. The tag is computed by the sender and is sent to the receiver, who recomputes the value to check that the data was not corrupted in transit, which attests the integrity of the data. Furthermore, MACs involve a shared-key between parties. So, Alice has the same MAC key as Bob. Therefore, when Bob verifies the MAC on a message, he is assured that the sender has the same MAC key as himself. In OTR, because Alice and Bob have the same MAC key that is applied to individual messages, either one of them can create messages to imitate the other. Therefore, neither of them can prove that they, nor their communicating partner, definitively produced a message. This provides the repudiation feature in OTR.

The OTR designers incorporate one additional unorthodox feature for a cryptographic system: forgeability. OTR is designed so that it is easy to change the ciphertext en route to produce a meaningful output when the message is decrypted. This can be performed because the designers chose a malleable encryption scheme using a stream cipher; in OTR's case, it uses AES-CTR with a 128-bit key length. In stream ciphers, the *meat* of the cipher is generating a key stream, but the actual encryption is typically performed by applying the exclusive-OR operation to the plaintext. Decryption is performed with the same exclusive-OR function applied to the same keystream. An attacker, who can guess the plaintext of the message, can modify the ciphertext to produce a different plaintext message of the same length. Therefore, the messages can be forged.

Exclusive-OR, or XOR, can be used for both encryption and decryption due to its logical definition: the XOR of A and B is true if and only if either A or B is true. Digital messages are represented as binary streams. The plaintext of a message is XORed with a key stream to produce a ciphertext, and when that ciphertext is XORed with the same key stream, the plaintext is returned. For example, if the plaintext bit is 1 and the key stream bit is 1, the ciphertext will return 0. When the ciphertext bit, 0, is applied to the keystream 1, the plaintext bit 1 is recovered. The Khan Academy has an interactive and visual series on XOR in cryptography: `https://www.khanacademy.org/computing/computer-science/cryptography/ciphers/a/xor-bitwise-operation`.

Alice and Bob are still protected from a third party, who doesn't know the MAC key, being able to tamper with their immediate conversation. However, OTR includes yet another twist. It publishes the MAC keys of the previous conversation once it has re-keyed to new MAC keys. Publishing the MAC keys means that anyone who has passively monitored the conversation can change the ciphertext, and thus, manipulate the plaintext of past messages. This adds another layer of deniability to the conversation, as any recorded conversation could be easily manipulated and might seem legitimate. Alice and Bob only publish *old* MAC keys, the key currently in use is kept secret until the protocol requires them to re-key.

On the usability of OTR

Designing cryptosystems is not enough to ensure their adoption; they also need to be robust and usable. OTR was not only published as an academic paper, but a library was provided as well. OTR was designed to work over any existing **Instant Message (IM)** protocol with any client that could incorporate the library, or plugin. Your favorite IRC client probably has a plugin or library that can easily incorporate OTR. In this chapter, we will be using OTR plugins that are built in the two IRC applications we will examine.

The design of OTR, specifically the perfect forward secrecy and deniability features, have inspired derivates for other protocols besides real-time chatting. For example, Open WhisperSystems' TextSecure app for mobile devices uses an OTR-like protocol over SMS and other asynchronous IM channels.

Also, OTR, like Tor and GPG, is recommended by the Freedom of the Press Foundation, a U.S. Non-profit organization that *supports and defends public interest journalism*. This organization provides education and tutorials on how to use these tools. While presented in the contexts of journalists protecting their sources, as Glenn Greenwald and Laura Poitras used (Greenwald 2014), the information is applicable to any user of privacy enhancing technology.

Using the BeagleBone to protect your online chats

In this chapter, we'll be using the BBB to run OTR on various IRC gateways. The BBB is well suited to act as your personal IRC gateway. It can easily handle the IRC connections and act as an always-on server without dramatically increasing your electric bill. While IRC may seem archaic, it provides an interface that is client independent and modular. We'll eventually build a complete IRC solution, one that manages all of your IRC networks. First we will look at the software BitlBee, which merges your chat networks like Google Talk and Jabber into IRC.

Installing BitlBee on the BeagleBone

BitlBee is an *IRC to-other-chat-networks gateway*. This means that if you use an existing chat program, such as Google Talk, Jabber, Twitter, AIM, or Facebook, you can use BitlBee to chat over those protocols via IRC. The first question when a non-IRC user hears about BitlBee is, *why would you want to do this?* while IRC users respond with excitement. The major benefit is that by using IRC, you can effectively chat with buddies over Google Talk using the same client software as you use to chat on IRC. This reduces the number of programs you have to learn. While this may not seem impressive at first, consider that each program typically has its own keyboard shortcuts and distinct interface. Also, each vendor frequently changes the appearance of their application, requiring you to re-learn how to use the tool. On the other hand, IRC clients are fairly simple in their user interface and IRC interactions are fairly standardized.

The other reason BitlBee is useful is that it acts as a proxy server for your chat networks. Your chat network presence is persistent but you can attach and detach your client at will. When you re-attach, you can catch-up on missed instant messages. This will prevent receiving a message on one client, like your phone, but missing it because you then logged into the chat network with your computer. Additionally, BitlBee supports OTR so we can use BitlBee to manage our OTR protected conversations.

BitlBee and the OTR plugin are available through the Debian repositories, so installing is as easy as:

```
sudo apt-get install bitlbee bitlbee-plugin-otr
```

The installation procedure will automatically start the BitlBee daemon running on port 6667, which is the default IRC port. At this point, you can connect with your favorite IRC client to your BitlBee server. This is one of the advantages of running BitlBee on your local network from a BBB, it's always on and available from any other internal computer or smartphone. Since BitlBee is marshalling your accounts, it won't appear as if you are coming online and offline.

In this chapter, the IRC client we will use will be ERC, which is the Emacs IRC client. ERC is a client that runs inside an Emacs instance and has several advantages over traditional IRC clients. First and most important, if you are already using Emacs, you can be more efficient if you can use Emacs for other tasks. Not only do you save the cognitive friction from task switching, but the layout and keyboard commands are already known to you. Also, ERC, like Emacs, is extremely modular and flexible. It is, of course, a free software program, but there are also many existing modules from nick highlighting to autoaway that you can use. Lastly, it's naturally cross-platform; any platform that can run Emacs can run ERC.

For Emacs users, running an IRC client in Emacs makes sense. After all, dedicated Emacs users consider Emacs to be the most portable operating system. If you insist on not using Emacs, irssi is a well-respected IRC client alternative: http://www.irssi.org/.

To connect to your BBB BitlBee server with ERC, inside Emacs, type M-x erc. You'll be prompted for the IP address. Then hit enter for the default port number and enter again for the password. You should join the &bitlbee channel and there will be one other user in that channel with you, root. The following screenshot shows how root interacts with you in the &bitlbee channel but also illustrates the IRC client interface inside Emacs:

```
○ ○ ○              Emacs Prelude – &bitlbee — (83 x 21)
jbd on &bitlbee (+Ct,lag:0) Welcome to the control channel. Type help for help informat
1
2
3
4 [Tue Jul  1 2014]
5 *** Users on &bitlbee: @jbd @root                                          [09:11]
6 *** Topic for &bitlbee: Welcome to the control channel. Type help for help
7     information.
8 *** &bitlbee: topic set by root!root@192.168.1.21, 2014-07-01 09:11:11
9 <root> Welcome to the BitlBee gateway!
10 <root>
11 <root> If you've never used BitlBee before, please do read the help
12        information using the help command. Lots of FAQs are answered there.
13 <root> If you already have an account on this server, just use the identify
14        command to identify yourself.
15 <root> The nick is (probably) not registered
16 *** &bitlbee modes: +Ct
17 ERC> ▮

-:**-  &bitlbee@BitlBee    All of 643  (17,5)     (ERC Projectile Fly Pre)
```

Creating a BitlBee account

The first task is to create an account on your BitlBee server. This is a new account that will manage your BitlBee connections. Later, we can log back in with this account to load our configuration. Otherwise, we would have to repeat the following steps each time we connect. Since BitlBee is an IRC gateway, all the commands to BitlBee have an IRC feel to them. Registration is performed by typing the following command in the &bitlbee channel:

```
register <password>
```

Your password will be echoed back to you and the root user should reply with:

```
Account successfully created
```

With BitlBee, it's important to get into the habit of saving often. Otherwise, changes are not persistent. Saving is simply done by typing save into the &bitlbee channel. Go ahead and save now.

Adding a Google Talk account to BitlBee

A BitlBee account alone is not that useful. We need to add your other social media accounts to BitlBee in order to make it useful. The first account we will add is a Google Talk account. BitlBee supports other chat services such as Yahoo, AIM, XMPP, MSN, Facebook, and Twitter, so you don't have to use a Google account. For the full list, refer to http://wiki.bitlbee.org/FrontPage.

Unfortunately, in May 2013, Google announced its new communications product *Hangouts*, which does not support XMPP, which is an IETF standard, but instead uses a proprietary protocol. Specifically, Google Hangout does not support server-to-server federation support with XMPP. If you have an independent XMPP server, or have an account on Jabber.org or the Free Software Foundation's server, it will no longer be possible to communicate with Google Hangout users. You can still use Google Talk, which fully supports XMPP, but it is not clear when Google will retire Google Talk.

> If you don't have a Google account, because of valid privacy concerns, you should read *Google has most of my e-mail because it has all of yours* by Benjamin Mako Hill http://mako.cc/copyrighteous/ google-has-most-of-my-email-because-it-has-all-of- yours. The author didn't use Gmail, but over 50 percent of his e-mails correspondence went to Google servers. Unless you are encrypting your e-mail, Google servers have your correspondence.

To add your Gmail account in BitlBee, type the following into the &bitlbee channel:

```
account add jabber you@gmail.com
```

The BitlBee root account will respond with:

```
<root> Account successfully added with tag gtalk
<root> You can now use the /OPER command to enter the password
<root> Alternatively, enable OAuth if the account supports it: account gtalk set oauth on
```

We'll go ahead and enable OAuth:

```
acc gtalk set oauth on
```

> OAuth is an *authorization framework* that allows third-party access to other web services without the need for the third-party application to know your credential, for example, password. Limited use access tokens are provided to the third-party application to restrict the access on the hosting service. More information is available on the OAuth website http://oauth.net.

As most people have Google+ accounts now, we have to set the format of the nicks to full names. Otherwise, we will see random strings as nicknames:

```
account gtalk set nick_format %full_name
```

Finally, enable the account with:

```
acc gtalk on
```

BitlBee will send a private message to a URL for your OAuth login:

```
<jabber_oauth> Open this URL in your browser to authenticate:
https://...
<jabber_oauth> Respond to this message with the returned authorization
token.
```

Clicking on the link will prompt you to accept BitlBee's permissions, which should look like the following screenshot. After clicking on **Accept**, you'll receive a code, which you can then paste back into the private message window.

Once complete, back in the `&bitlbee` window, you should see the following messages indicating you are logging in to GTalk:

```
<root> jabber - Logging in: Starting OAuth authentication
<root> jabber - Logging in: Requesting OAuth access token
<root> jabber - Logging in: Connecting
<root> jabber - Logging in: Connected to server, logging in
<root> jabber - Logging in: Converting stream to TLS
<root> jabber - Logging in: Connected to server, logging in
<root> jabber - Logging in: Authentication finished
<root> jabber - Logging in: Server changed session resource string to
`BitlBee301D65C5'
<root> jabber - Logging in: Authenticated, requesting buddy list
```

```
<root> jabber - Logging in: Logged in
```

Don't forget to save!

Adding a Jabber account to BitlBee

If you have a Jabber (XMPP) account, you can go ahead and add that to Bitlbee. The syntax is similar to the prior example:

```
account add jabber username@jabber.org password
```

The root user should return with something like:

```
Account successfully added with tag jabber
```

Turn the account on with:

```
acc jabber on
```

You should now see two accounts when you type `account list`. Lastly, save your data!

 You can add your Twitter account as well and tweet from IRC. However, you'll need BitlBee version 3.2.1 or greater; otherwise, you will receive SSL errors when trying to connect to twitter.

One of the many benefits of joining the Free Software Foundation as a member is the use of the FSF's XMPP server. Through federation, users can reach you at your FSF username at the member.fsf.org server. Similarly, fellows of the Free Software Foundation Europe also have XMPP privileges. For more information, visit the respective FSF sites at `https://www.fsf.org/associate/benefits` and `https://fsfe.org/fellowship/index.en.html`, respectively.

Adding OTR to your BitlBee server

We installed the OTR plugin for BitlBee already, so it's ready to support OTR. Prior to an encrypted conversation, we must first generate a key pair. For each account you have registered with BitlBee, you can have unique key pairs. View your account list and then generate an OTR key with:

```
otr keygen 0
```

After a few seconds, root will inform you that OTR key generation is complete. At any point, you can view information on your OTR keys with:

```
otr info
```

This will provide the key fingerprints for each account. You are now ready to have an encrypted chat.

Managing contacts in BitlBee

Your contacts, or buddy list, should have been available when BitlBee authenticated your account. You can view your buddy list in the `&bitlbee` window with the `blist` command. This table will show the nick, the handle at the specific account, and the status of each contact. BitlBee converts the handle into IRC-friendly names, which are the "nicks" in the first column. It can become confusing when people use the same handle on separate accounts. BitlBee allows you to rename nicks to help manage this problem. For example, BitlBee will append duplicate nicks with an underscore, but you can rename them with the following command:

```
rename gabriel_ice_ gabriel_ice_jabber
```

Adding contacts is also straightforward with the familiar command syntax:

```
add 0 gabriel.ice@gmail.com
```

Just remember to check your account list to know which account number to use.

Chatting with BitlBee

Chatting can be performed directly in the `&bitlbee` channel. Use IRC syntax to specify the nick and BitlBee will direct it to the appropriate service. A basic chat session, between `maxine` and `gabriel_ice_japper`, would look like this:

```
<maxine> gabriel_ice_jabber: when can we meet to talk about DeepArcher?

<gabriel_ice_jabber> maxine: Tuesday at 10.
```

Alternatively, you can use the `/query` command to open a new window and chat directly with the user. With this method, you don't have to specify the user's nick each time because you and your buddy are in a private chat.

> For those new to IRC, the following tutorial is a good introduction: `http://www.irchelp.org/irchelp/irctutorial.html`. For those looking for ERC-specific help, the Emacs Wiki has some resources: `http://www.emacswiki.org/emacs/ErcBasics`.

Chatting with OTR in BitlBee

To initiate an OTR protected chat, type:

```
otr connect gabriel_ice_jabber
```

While we are connected at this point and the chat session will be encrypted, we are left with the problem of how do we really know who we are chatting with? This question may seem existential, but it is an important one. A common attack on a communication protocol is a **Man-In-The-Middle (MITM)** attack. The canonical setup of the MITM attack involves two parties who wish to communicate, Alice and Bob, and the malicious meddler Mallory. Alice initiates a connection with Bob, but it is usurped by Mallory and likewise with the connection from Bob to Alice. Alice thinks she is talking to Bob, but really she is talking to Mallory, who is forwarding messages to Bob and vice versa. At this point, Mallory can direct and manipulate the conversation at will.

To defeat this, we need to authenticate the receiving party. In OTR, you could verify the key fingerprint of your partner. This requires you to have swapped OTR fingerprints *a priori* and it might not be very convenient to carry your OTR fingerprint with you at all times. The other mechanism is to use the **Socialist Millionaire Problem** to authenticate your buddy. The Socialist Millionaire Problem is discussed in more detail in the following subsection, for now, think of it as a question and answer game where the answer would only be known by the person with whom you are communicating.

To initiate the protocol in BitlBee, type something like the following:

```
otr smpq gabriel_ice_jabber "What beer did I order last night, one word,
lowercase?" ipa
```

Presumably, you and Gabriel Ice were out at dinner last night and he would know the type of beer you ordered. When phrasing the question, it's good to include instructions of how to type it. Else, it would result in an incorrect response and probably confuse your partner, who despite the drinks, distinctly remembers you drinking an IPA. If your partner responds correctly, you should see:

```
<root> smp: initiating with gabriel_ice_jabber_...
```

```
<root> smp gabriel_ice_jabber_: secrets proved equal, fingerprint trusted
```

This mechanism is one-way; Gabriel must initiate the protocol in order to fully trust you as well. This portion of the exchange looks like this:

```
<root> smp: initiated by gabriel_ice_jabber with question: "What did I
have for lunch yesterday, one word, lowercase?"
```

```
<root> smp: respond with otr smp gabriel_ice_jabber <answer>
```

```
<jbd> otr smp gabriel_ice_jabber pizza
<root> smp: responding to gabriel_ice_jabber...
<root> smp gabriel_ice_jabber: correct answer, you are trusted
```

Congratulations! You have connected and authenticated and may chat away with OTR and BitlBee! If you are using GTalk and are also logged in to Google with your browser, you may notice the encrypted messages going back and forth. You can probably log out of GTalk from your browser, but just for fun, if you are logged in, you will see the OTR messages, which look like this:

```
?OTR:AAIDAAAAAAQAAAAFAAAAwBPAdyxNJT7MYxOFBPfmPRCbW3yE6gADfimB7wikaf
/r9/DVQ3hZfJXj+c7HSddySk77fJi3csbRIIxKCSXGLO/9cOw7SJ+u10d8D6Wp2scCAi7TzO
/YGkZmeGlef31YUbwaVkH5VoYfLSo+i90McmLrgEfM9kgZuXLtDA1H2f4jWdtBJh1XxdK
/GyZBZvTcncMs/e3rRrKpSNZiJq0kijMhIK6N4NRdaNK1URipDJai1d2bnGJ2Pk0rihXc5yzCr
gAAAAAAAAACAAAAEUw6xZ+tJrdEG/+yqaiwoDi0Fc9eloiWtIc1UWQ8JTIT3eaKvuMAAAA.
```

Understanding the Socialist Millionaire Problem

Even a well-designed protocol such as OTR can have subtle design flaws. For those looking to add cryptography to your project, there is a well-known saying, *don't roll your own crypto*, which means don't invent your own cryptography because the odds are against you and one mistake can undermine your security. Plus even seasoned cryptographers don't get everything right on the first try. Fortunately, releasing the research, design, and code helps with the peer review process.

In response to some critiques on OTR's authentication phase, the authors improved their protocol (Alexander 2007). Prior to this paper, OTR users had to verify the fingerprint of OTR keys out-of-band. While this works, it has a human factor drawback as it is inconvenient and not very scalable to hand out OTR keys to people with whom you may want to securely communicate. However, two parties may share more intimate knowledge about each other that would prove their authenticity. The problem then becomes how do Alice and Bob share some secret information without revealing it to each other. The researchers discovered that this problem is a re-statement of the Socialist Millionaire Problem where two millionaires want to know whether they are equally wealthy without revealing to each other the quantity of their wealth.

The mathematics behind this problem rely on a technique called a **zero-knowledge proof**. A zero knowledge proof allows someone to attest to the correctness of a statement without providing any additional information about the said statement. The details and proof of OTR's zero-knowledge proofs are beyond the scope of this book and described in detail in (Alexander 2007).

The implication of using the Socialist Millionaire Problem in OTR is that Alice can ask Bob a specific question that only Bob would know. If Mallory is masquerading as Bob and if Alice chose a good question to which Mallory doesn't know the answer, Mallory won't gain any additional information about the answer if she guesses wrong. For example, Alice asks Mallory, pretending to be Bob, who her favorite guitarist is. Bob knows that Alice is a *Who* fan and the answer is none other then Pete Townshend. Mallory does not know this detail so she provides an admirable, but incorrect, answer of Jimmy Page. Alice will see the protocol fail and know that Bob is not who he appears to be. But Mallory will not know any other information about the answer other than that Jimmy Page is not correct. However, it is too late for Mallory because Alice no longer trusts her and terminates the connection.

Marshalling your IRC connections with a Bouncer

Now that BitlBee is running on the BeagleBone, you can enjoy OTR-protected instant messaging, but we can improve the setup. Currently, we are connecting to BitlBee directly from your IRC client. This is fine if you have one client. But, if you are chatting with your laptop and then get up and go, you may want to continue a conversation on your phone. For this, we will need a more persistent proxy connection. The problem can be stated in a more general way: how can we maintain a persistent connection to all of our IRC networks, including BitlBee. For this, we'll need an IRC bouncer.

IRC bouncers act as a proxy server and maintain your connection to an IRC server. This may be useful on servers that don't support nick registration and you want to maintain your nick. As mentioned in the previous use case, bouncers generally support multiple clients which will allow you to have a near seamless IRC conversation as you switch devices. Since we are using BitlBee as an IRC gateway to our XMPP and instant message networks, we can combine IRC connections as well and have all of this managed by the bouncer.

The modern uses of IRC

IRC was invented in 1988 and it was one of the first global, real-time, chat networks. While social networks may have replaced much of the casual conversation on the Internet, IRC still has its place. While those conversations still continue on IRC, there is a group that routinely hangs out on IRC that should be of interest to the readers of this book: open source developers. Most well-maintained open source projects have a corresponding IRC channel where at all hours, you can generally find help.

For open source projects, the two biggest IRC networks are **freenode** and **oftc**. In fact, every major software and hardware package in this book has a corresponding IRC channel where you can ask for help. There are a few benefits to using IRC over other mediums. For active channels, it is beneficial and encouraged to **lurk** prior to adding to the conversation. Lurking is just passively watching the conversation. You may, and probably will, learn something just by reading the existing conversation. Also, if you do have a problem or a question, IRC is a real-time chat, so you potentially can quickly resolve your issue. It's also a more informal medium than a public mailing list. If you have some trepidation about asking your question on a mailing list, IRC is the place to ask.

On freenode, the relevant channels are: #sparkfun, for general electronics questions and to chat with some SparkFun employees and customers, #beagle, home to BeagleBone enthusiasts, #gnupg, for GPG-related questions, and #cryptotronix, which is the author's channel about open source crypto hardware. On oftc (irc.oftc.net), you can check out the #bitlbee channel for help on BitlBee or #tor to talk about Tor.

IRC, like any shared communication medium, has certain **netiquette** that users expect everyone to follow. Surprisingly, there is an RFC that defines netiquette guidelines (RFC 1855). It's certainly worth a read, but you should be ok if you follow these tips. First of all, *don't ask to ask*. This means, don't ask in an IRC channel if you can ask a question. You can just ask your question directly. While there are operators in channels, IRC typically doesn't follow the raise-your-hand-and-wait-to-be-called-on approach. Secondly, don't *flood* the channel. This means not to paste a large amount of text into the channel as it will cause all connected clients to rapidly scroll the text off of the screen. Instead, use a paste service like that provided by Debian (http://paste.debian.net/) and then paste the link in the IRC channel, while explaining what is contained in the linked information. Lastly, be patient. As previously stated, many people lurk on IRC in the background and may not immediately see your question. Depending on the time at which you asked your question, it's reasonable to wait 30 minutes or so. On an active channel, you'll probably get a response quicker than that, just don't keep asking the question repeatedly.

Downloading and installing the IRC bouncer ZNC

We'll be using the IRC bouncer package called ZNC. ZNC is a well-maintained and up-to-date package and like all good open source software, has an IRC channel: `#znc` on freenode. The packages in the Debian repository are a bit old, so we'll install ZNC from source. Download the source tarball by issuing the following command:

`wget http://znc.in/releases/znc-1.4.tar.gz`

We want to develop the good habit of checking signatures on downloaded software. The 1.4 release is signed by Alexey Sokolov, whose GPG fingerprint is: `D582 3CAC B477 191C AC00 7555 5AE4 20CC 0209 989E`. You can download his public key with the following command:

`gpg -recv-key  D5823CACB477191CAC0075555AE420CC0209989E`

Next, download the signature file for the release:

`wget http://znc.in/releases/znc-1.4.tar.gz.sig`

Lastly, verify the signature over the downloaded software:

```
gpg --verify znc-1.4.tar.gz.sig znc-1.4.tar.gz
```
```
You should see something like the following:
```
```
gpg: Signature made Thu 08 May 2014 08:21:40 PM UTC using RSA key ID
0209989E
```
```
gpg: Good signature from "Alexey Sokolov <alexey@alexeysokolov.co.cc>"
```
```
gpg:                 aka "Alexey Sokolov <ktonibud@gmail.com>"
```
```
gpg:                 aka "Alexey Sokolov <alexey@asokolov.org>"
```
```
gpg: WARNING: This key is not certified with a trusted signature!
```
```
gpg:          There is no indication that the signature belongs to the
owner.
```
```
Primary key fingerprint: D582 3CAC B477 191C AC00  7555 5AE4 20CC 0209
989E
```

While this procedure adds a few steps, it should soon become second nature. If you don't perform these steps, when there is a signature file available, you are assuming that the software you downloaded is the software that was posted. Even though there are checksums built into the TCP, which you are using when you use `wget`, it does not guarantee that the file is the correct file since there is an opportunity for a MITM attack. Regardless of your paranoia level, it's good practice to verify the software each time. In fact, a quick bash script will help here since it's standard practice to append `.sig` to the end of the file:

```
wgetsig(){
    wget $1
    wget $1.sig
    fn=$(basename $1)
    gpg --verify $fn.sig $fn
}
```

If you add that function to your `.bashrc` or equivalent, you can just type `wgetsig` `<url>` to grab the file, the signature, and run them through GPG. Now that you can trust that the software you downloaded is the software that was posted, you can finally extract the package:

tar -zxvf znc-1.4.tar.gz

To build ZNC from source, you'll want to install the following dependencies:

sudo apt-get install libssl-dev libperl-dev

Most software tarballs support the `confgure-make-make install` dance and this one is no different. You can build and install with the following:

cd znc-*

./configure

make

sudo make install

Building ZNC on the BBB will take a while because it will build each of the ZNC modules as well, so go enjoy some coffee.

Configure ZNC to manage your IRC connections

Before we configure ZNC, let's step back and examine our system architecture. We have at least three distinct pieces of hardware involved: the machine on which your IRC client is running, the BBB, and the machines running IRC servers. One of those machines is the BBB since it's running the BitlBee IRC server. Examine the following deployment diagram:

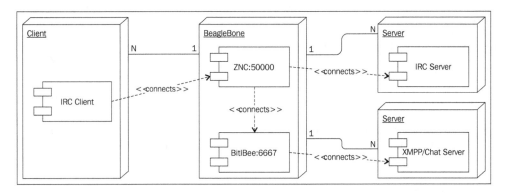

Let's start with the BBB, depicted by the center cube. The BBB is running two modules: ZNC and BitlBee. ZNC is the module to which multiple IRC clients can connect. ZNC is connected to the BitlBee module, which is a process also running on the same hardware. ZNC is also connected to one or more different IRC servers. BitlBee maintains connections to various XMPP or chat servers but since BitlBee itself is an IRC server, you connect to it through ZNC. Once everything is set up, you will only have to worry about connecting to ZNC.

ZNC needs a configuration file and the easiest way to generate the configuration file is to run the following command:

```
znc --makeconf
```

This will launch an interactive command-line interface. You'll need to create a new ZNC username that is not associated with any BitlBee or IRC systems. You will also have to decide what port to run the service. If you pick a port number in the private range, 49152 to 65535, you'll have less of a chance of colliding with another service. For this example, port 50000 was chosen. There are quite a few ZNC modules, but you'll want to enable the webadmin module to easily configure ZNC. Lastly, be sure to enable SSL. It will generate a self-signed certificate, at which most browsers will grumble when connecting. Alternatively, you can create a full **Public Key Infrastructure (PKI)**, complete with your own certificate authority, and supply the server certificate to ZNC.

PKIs are a bookworthy subtopic. An introduction to the complexities to PKI is well documented by Peter Gutmann in *Everything you Never Wanted to Know about PKI but were Forced to Find Out* at http://www.cs.auckland.ac.nz/~pgut001/pubs/pkitutorial.pdf.

The example configuration session is listed as follows:

```
[ .. ] Checking for list of available modules...
[ >> ] ok
[ ** ] Building new config
[ ** ]
[ ** ] First let's start with some global settings...
[ ** ]
[ ?? ] What port would you like ZNC to listen on? (1025 to 65535): 50000
[ ?? ] Would you like ZNC to listen using SSL? (yes/no) [no]: yes
[ ?? ] Would you like ZNC to listen using both IPv4 and IPv6? (yes/no)
[yes]: yes
[ .. ] Verifying the listener...
[ >> ] ok
[ ** ] Unable to locate pem file: [/home/debian/.znc/znc.pem], creating
it
[ .. ] Writing Pem file [/home/debian/.znc/znc.pem]...
[ >> ] ok
[ ** ]
[ ** ] -- Global Modules --
[ ** ]
[ ** ] +----------+-------------------------------------------------
-----+
[ ** ] | Name     | Description
[ ** ] +----------+-------------------------------------------+
[ ** ] | partyline | Internal channels and queries for users
                                       connected to znc |
[ ** ] | webadmin  | Web based administration module           |
[ ** ] +----------+-------------------------------------------+
[ ** ] And 10 other (uncommon) modules. You can enable those
       later.
[ ** ]
[ ?? ] Load global module <partyline>? (yes/no) [no]: yes
[ ?? ] Load global module <webadmin>? (yes/no) [no]: yes
[ ** ]
```

```
[ ** ] Now we need to set up a user...
[ ** ]
[ ?? ] Username (AlphaNumeric): zncbeagle
[ ?? ] Enter Password:
[ ?? ] Confirm Password:
[ ?? ] Would you like this user to be an admin? (yes/no) [yes]:
       yes
[ ?? ] Nick [zncbeagle]:
[ ?? ] Alt Nick [zncbeagle_]:
[ ?? ] Ident [zncbeagle]:
[ ?? ] Real Name [Got ZNC?]: ZNC Admin
[ ?? ] Bind Host (optional):
[ ?? ] Number of lines to buffer per channel [50]:
[ ?? ] Would you like to clear channel buffers after replay?
       (yes/no) [yes]:
[ ?? ] Default channel modes [+stn]:
[ ** ]
[ ** ] -- User Modules --
[ ** ]
[ ** ] +--------------+---------------------------------------------+
[ ** ] | Name         | Description                                 |
[ ** ] +--------------+---------------------------------------------+
[ ** ] | chansaver    | Keep config up-to-date when user            |
       |              | joins/parts                                 |
[ ** ] | controlpanel | Dynamic configuration through IRC. Allows editing
only yourself if you're not ZNC admin. |
[ ** ] | perform      | Keeps a list of commands to be executed when ZNC
connects to IRC.                  |
[ ** ] | webadmin     | Web based administration module             |
       |
[ ** ] +--------------+---------------------------------------------
--------------------------------------+
[ ** ] And 21 other (uncommon) modules. You can enable those later.
[ ** ]
[ ?? ] Load module <chansaver>? (yes/no) [no]:
[ ?? ] Load module <controlpanel>? (yes/no) [no]:
[ ?? ] Load module <perform>? (yes/no) [no]:
[ ?? ] Load module <webadmin>? (yes/no) [no]: yes
[ ** ]
[ ?? ] Would you like to set up a network? (yes/no) [no]:
```

```
[ ** ]
[ ?? ] Would you like to set up another user? (yes/no) [no]:
[ .. ] Writing config [/home/debian/.znc/configs/znc.conf]...
[ >> ] ok
[ ** ]
[ ** ]To connect to this ZNC you need to connect to it as your IRC server
[ ** ]using the port that you supplied.  You have to supply your login
info
[ ** ]as the IRC server password like this: user/network:pass.
[ ** ]
[ ** ]Try something like this in your IRC client...
[ ** ]/server <znc_server_ip> +50000 zncbeagle:<pass>
[ ** ]And this in your browser...
[ ** ]https://<znc_server_ip>:50000/
[ ** ]
[ ?? ] Launch ZNC now? (yes/no) [yes]: yes
[ .. ] Opening config [/home/debian/.znc/configs/znc.conf]...
[ >> ] ok
[ .. ] Loading global module [partyline]...
[ >> ] [/usr/local/lib/znc/partyline.so]
[ .. ] Loading global module [webadmin]...
[ >> ] [/usr/local/lib/znc/webadmin.so]
[ .. ] Binding to port [+50000]...
[ >> ] ok
[ ** ] Loading user [zncbeagle]
[ .. ] Loading user module [webadmin]...
[ >> ] [/usr/local/lib/znc/webadmin.so]
[ .. ] Forking into the background...
[ >> ] [pid: 7019]
[ ** ] ZNC 1.4 - http://znc.in
```

Adding OTR to your ZNC server

While BitlBee has our XMPP and chat networks covered with OTR, our IRC networks are OTR-less at the moment. If you don't plan on using OTR, then you can still use the BBB as your IRC gateway and enjoy a consolidated IRC platform. Since OTR has to be initiated by one of the communicating parties, this chat configuration will interoperate with any IRC system. But, if you want OTR over your other IRC channels, then there are two methods to resolve this. First of all, you can use OTR from your IRC client. This will provide an end-to-end OTR session from your client to your communicating party, assuming they are using OTR from their client. However, most, but not all clients have an OTR-plugin. The other approach, the one that will be presented here, is to use OTR inside ZNC.

There are pros and cons to this approach. The benefit is that for all of your chat networks, regardless of your client, you will have the same OTR key. Therefore, once your buddies authenticate you and trust your key, they can keep that trust even when you switch to a different IRC network. Also, you will no longer need to run an OTR plugin on your client. However, the OTR session is terminated at ZNC. Therefore, it is extremely important to have a secure connection from your client to ZNC. At minimum, you should turn on the SSL option as previously mentioned. With that self-signed certificate, you are susceptible to a MITM attack, though, so it may be worth your time to generate a certificate authority and issue a certificate to your ZNC server. The reason you are at risk is that it's fairly easy to generate a self-signed certificate as ZNC does. At minimum, you should take note of the public key generated in the self-signed certificate and only trust the SSL connection if your ZNC server presents that known key. This technique is known as **certificate pinning**. As previously mentioned, generating PKIs is a nuanced task, so I'll leave this as a (moderately difficult) exercise for the reader.

Another option, if you don't want to deal with SSL, is that you can `ssh` into your BBB and run an IRC client on localhost. This will still provide confidentiality for your messages between your computer and the server (the BBB) but it will restrict the IRC clients available to you since the IRC client would be running on the BBB. For the rest of this chapter, we will continue with the SSL approach.

The ZNC OTR module is fairly new, so it must be built from source. It also depends on a version of OTR that is not available in Debian wheezy, but it is available as a backport. Edit your apt-sources file to add the backport repository:

```
sudo nano /etc/apt/sources.list
```

Add the following line to the end:

```
deb http://http.debian.net/debian wheezy-backports main
```

Then perform:

```
sudo apt-get update
```

To install the newer version of OTR, enter the following command:

```
sudo apt-get -t wheezy-backports install "libotr5" "libotr5-dev"
```

Clone the `znc-otr` module repository:

```
git clone https://github.com/mmilata/znc-otr.git
```

Enter the directory and type `make`. You should see:

```
LIBS="-lotr" znc-buildmod otr.cpp
Building "otr.so" for ZNC 1.4... [ ok ]
```

Copy `otr.so` to `~/.znc/modules` and note, you may have to create the modules directory. The `znc-otr` module is now installed, but not loaded.

Adding your networks to ZNC

With all of the components installed, we can now configure ZNC. Since we've enabled the ZNC `webadmin` module, we can use our browser to configure our bouncer and add accounts. You can access the `webadmin` module by typing the URL of your BBB followed by the port number of ZNC as follows:

```
https://192.168.1.42:50000
```

Log in with your username and password. On the right-hand side of the page, there will be a navigation menu as shown in the following screenshot:

Click on **Your Settings**. Then scroll down to the **Networks** section and click on **Add**. Here you can add your BitlBee settings we previously created. The **Network Name** is BitlBee and the **Nickname** is the BitlBee user you created. Under **Servers of this IRC Network**, enter the following and replace the password with your BitlBee password:

```
localhost 6667 password
```

Scroll to the bottom of the page and click on **Add Network** to save. Now you can go back to the **Your Settings** page and add other IRC networks in a similar manner. For this chapter, let's add a freenode account as we'll be using it to demonstrate how to use OTR over IRC. If you don't have one, you can make up a nick and enter the following in the **Servers of this IRC network** section:

```
chat.freenode.net +6697
```

The +6697 indicates to ZNC that you want to connect to freenode using SSL on port 6697, which is the semi-official IRC TLS port. You can add channels by clicking on Add under **Channels** and ZNC will not only keep you in the channel when your client detaches, but will playback the channel's conversation. You can specify how many lines to playback by changing the **Buffer Count** setting in the **Channel Info** screen.

Connecting to ZNC from your IRC client

You can now connect to ZNC from your IRC client. Depending on the client, you should be able to set your username and password in the `server password` field. If you receive an *incorrect password* warning and you are sure that you typed in the password correctly, set your password to `username:password`. You need to do this if using ERC. More specifically, you should connect with `M-x erc-tls` and supply the IP of your BBB, the port number of ZNC, username, and the password in the previous format.

If you've added multiple networks, the first messages you should see are the following when you make your connection to your BBB:

```
-*status- You have several networks configured, but no network was
specified for the connection.
-*status- Selecting network [bitlbee]. To see list of all configured
networks, use /znc ListNetworks
-*status- If you want to choose another network, use /znc JumpNetwork
<network>, or connect to ZNC with username zncbeagle/<network> (instead
of just zncbeagle)
```

These messages are from a **virtual user**. The prefix for virtual users is an `*` and this user is `status`. While ZNC is connected to multiple networks, you are only seeing the BitlBee network at the moment. Here you can interact with BitlBee like we did in a previous section. As long as ZNC and BitlBee are running, ZNC will remain connected to BitlBee and you can attach and detach at will. To use OTR on an actual IRC network, like freenode, we need to attach ZNC to the other network. There are two ways to do this. We can, as `status` reminded us, jump to that network with the following command, assuming you named your freenode network *freenode*:

```
/msg *status JumpNetwork freenode
```

This will take your existing session and *jump* it over to freenode. While you may be in the same client window, you are now talking on a different IRC network since we switched from BitlBee to freenode. If you use GNU screen or tmux, we just performed a similar action as we would have had we switched to a new screen. The session is still running; we are just looking at a different instance. This method has the benefit of only using one connection from your client to ZNC, but it can be a bit confusing.

Alternatively, you can open another ZNC connection. To indicate to ZNC that you want the new session to attach to a different network, you must use a different syntax. Your username must be in the form `username/network` and if you were sending the username in the password field, as you must with ERC, the format is `username/network:password`. So, in this example the username is:

```
zncbeagle/freenode
```

Using either method, connect to freenode via IRC.

Establishing OTR connections through ZNC

Now that we are using ZNC to manage our IRC traffic, let's establish an OTR session. The process is similar to what we did with BitlBee and by the end of this, you should be well-versed in establishing identity with OTR. For this experiment, you will either need a crypto-savy friend, a begrudging significant other, or a separate IRC account. Basically, you need somebody with whom you can chat via OTR.

Now that you are logged onto freenode or your favorite IRC network, initiate a chat with another user. On most clients, this will open the conversation in a new window when you type the following command:

```
/query username
```

At this point, you can enjoy an old-fashioned, unencrypted chat with your buddy. To chat with OTR, we first need to generate a key, like we did with BitlBee. In ZNC, there is a virtual user, *otr, similar to the *status user, to whom you direct OTR commands. First, you should generate a keypair by typing in the following command:

```
/msg *otr genkey
```

Remember, all virtual users in ZNC have the * prefix. This will probably open a new window with the *otr user and you should see something like this:

```
<*otr> Starting key generation in a background thread.
```

```
<*otr> Key generation finished.
```

Now you can initiate an OTR conversation. If you want to initiate the OTR conversation, type the following:

```
?OTR?
```

Otherwise, your buddy can initiate the OTR conversation and ZNC-OTR will automatically proceed with the protocol. Unlike BitlBee, the question is not part of the authenticate command, so you must type that first on your own. If Alice and Bob are talking, the conversation prior to the authenticate step would look like:

```
<alice> When prompted, answer the question: What was printed on my
t-shirt which I wore yesterday? One word, lowercase.
```

```
<bob> got it.
```

The command to initiate authentication is of the format: /msg *otr auth username answer. Continuing our example, the command would look like the following, where the answer to the question is *tworkeffx*:

```
/msg *otr auth bob tworkeffx
```

This will prompt your buddy to participate in the OTR authentication phase and what he sees on his screen depends on the IRC client he is using. The *otr user should respond with something like the following messages:

```
<*otr> [bob] Gone SECURE. Please make sure logging is turned off on your IRC

<*otr> [bob] Peer is not authenticated. There are two ways of verifying their identity:

<*otr> [bob] 1. Agree on a common secret (do not type it into the chat), then type auth bob <secret>.

<*otr> [bob] 2. Compare their fingerprint over a secure channel, then type trust bob.

<*otr> [bob] Your fingerprint:  E8949490 D0326A85 1049EE79 DF111C0A BCC68D42

<*otr> [bob] Their fingerprint: 00694775 3945FA05 B2E0DA61 5416DFFC 4F9C5936

<*otr> [bob] Initiated authentication.

<*otr> [bob] Peer replied to authentication request.

<*otr> [bob] Successfully authenticated.
```

As *otr reminds us, there are two methods to authenticate the user. We are using method number 1, which is the Socialist Millionaire Protocol. Your buddy, Bob, responded with your answer and you have authenticated him. Bob should conduct a similar exchange and the format for the answer is:

```
/msg *otr auth bob <answer>
```

And now, you can enjoy an encrypted chat session.

Extending the project

Currently, your BeagleBone is only serving your local network. You can enable port forwarding, like you did with your Tor server to open it up to the Internet to allow access to ZNC while you are on-the-go. If you do this, be sure that you are using SSL and consider using a Dynamic DNS service so you don't have to remember your IP address.

The ZNC and BitlBee packages are quite extensible. Moreover, since they are IRC servers, you can run an IRC **bot** in your ZNC server. There are several popular IRC bot packages and perhaps the most well known is Eggdrop (`http://www.eggheads.org/`). A custom bot on your BBB IRC server can interact with you from IRC to hardware. For example, if you add a temperature sensor on your BBB, you can query the bot to find out the temperature in the room. If you add a ZigBee radio to your BBB and attach the same temperature sensor to a corresponding ZigBee radio outside, powered by a battery, the bot can tell you the temperature outside. If you become an avid IRC user, you will enjoy combining the hardware electronics project with your BBB bot.

If you want to involve the CryptoCape to add some hardware protection, you could store ZNC's SSL certificate in the TPM. The TPM can store RSA keys and the keys can be generated such that the private key remains in the TPM. While there would be significant programming to connect the various components, this would certainly be a fun and challenging project!

Summary

In this chapter, you learned how to use another privacy tool, OTR. We used OTR with two different applications and examined how OTR authentication works. We also have our BBB set up to act as an IRC gateway to our chat networks and to manage all of our IRC communication.

In this book, we've taken three of the most popular and well-respected privacy and security applications and used them on the BeagleBone Black. The small form factor, low power consumption, and extendibility of the BBB makes it an ideal privacy aid. The software and hardware used in this book makes heavy use of cryptography, which is inherently a social and often controversial technology. We've also learned some of modern cryptography's social-political struggles along the way. Finally, you don't need to be a secret agent to communicate privately and securely; the best tools are freely available. You can improve these tools by using them and providing your feedback to the developers.

Happy hacking!

Selected Bibliography

Chapter 1

- Gibb, Alicia. "The death of patents and what comes after." Accessed September 3, 2014. https://www.youtube.com/watch?v=z__Sbw1Ax4o. TEDx Stockholm, 2012.

- BeagleBone Black Wiki. "WIFI Adapters." Accessed September 3, 2014. http://elinux.org/Beagleboard:BeagleBoneBlack#WIFI_Adapters.

- Batsov, Bozhidar. "Package Management in Emacs: The Good, the Bad and the Ugly." Accessed September 3, 2014. http://batsov.com/articles/2012/02/19/package-management-in-emacs-the-good-the-bad-and-the-ugly/. 2012.

- Batsov, Bozhidar. "Prelude." Accessed September 3, 2014. https://github.com/bbatsov/prelude. 2014.

- Cygwin. Accessed September 3, 2014. https://www.cygwin.com.

- Boneh, Dan. "Cryptography I." Accessed September 3, 2014. https://www.coursera.org/course/crypto.

- Boneh, Dan. "Cryptography II." Accessed September 3, 2014. https://www.coursera.org/course/crypto2.

- Molloy, Derek. "Setting up a C++ Cross-Development Platform." Accessed September 3, 2014. http://derekmolloy.ie/beaglebone/ setting-up-eclipse-on-the-beaglebone-for-c-development/. 2013.

- edX. "Introduction to Linux." Accessed September 3, 2014. https://www.edx.org/course/linuxfoundationx/linuxfoundationx-lfs101x-introduction-1621.

- eLinux Wiki. "BeagleBone Black Serial." Accessed September 3, 2014. http://elinux.org/Beagleboard:BeagleBone_Black_Serial.

- EmacsWiki. "Emacs Newbie." Accessed September 3, 2014. `http://www.emacswiki.org/emacs/EmacsNewbie`.

- EmacsWiki. "Viper Mode." Accessed September 3, 2014. `http://www.emacswiki.org/emacs/ViperMode`. 2014.

- Corey, Gerald. "BeagleBone Black System Reference Manual. Beagleboard.org." Accessed September 3, 2014. `https://github.com/CircuitCo/BeagleBone-Black/ blob/master/BBB_SRM.pdf?raw=true`. 2014.

- Hertzog, Raphael, and Roland Mas. *The Debian Administrator's Handbook*. Freexian SARL. 2013.

- Homebrew. Accessed September 3, 2014. `http://brew.sh/`.

- Axelson, Jan. "Using Eclipse to Cross-compile Applications for Embedded Systems." Accessed September 3, 2014. `http://janaxelson.com/eclipse1.htm`. 2014.

- Katz, Jonathan. "Cryptography." Accessed September 3, 2014. `https://www.coursera.org/course/cryptography`.

- Katz, Jonathan, and Yehuda Lindell. *Introduction to Modern Cryptography (Chapman & Hall/Crc Cryptography and Network Security Series)*. Chapman & Hall/CRC. 2007.

- Khan Academy. "Electricity and magnetism." Accessed September 3, 2014. `https://www.khanacademy.org/science/physics/electricity-and-magnetism`.

- Khan Academy. "Journey into cryptography." Accessed September 3, 2014. `https://www.khanacademy.org/computing/computer-science/cryptography`.

- Murphy, Sean, and Fred Piper. *Cryptography: A Very Short Introduction*. Oxford University Press. 2002.

- nixCraft. "Ubuntu / Debian Linux Regenerate OpenSSH Host Keys." Accessed September 3, 2014. `http://www.cyberciti.biz/faq/howto-regenerate-openssh-host-keys/`.

- Nmap.org. "Microsoft Windows binaries." Accessed September 3, 2014. `http://nmap.org/download.html#windows`.

- OSHWA. `http://www.oshwa.org/definition/`. 2013.

- Paar, Christof, and Jan Pelzl. *Understanding Cryptography: A Textbook for Students and Practitioners*. Springer Publishing Company, Incorporated. 2009.

- Munroe, Randall. "Permanence." Accessed September 3, 2014. `https://xkcd.com/910/`. 2008.

- Munroe, Randall. "Real Programmers." Accessed September 3, 2014. `https://xkcd.com/378/`. 2008.

- Chua, Sacha. "How to Learn Emacs." Accessed September 3, 2014. `http://sachachua.com/blog/wp-content/uploads/2013/05/How-to-Learn-Emacs-v2-Large.png`. 2013.

- Scherz, Paul. *Practical Electronics for Inventors*. McGraw-Hill. 3rd edition. 2013.

- Stallman, Richard M. "Emacs the extensible, customizable self-documenting display editor." *In Proceedings of the ACM SIGPLAN SIGOA Symposium on Text Manipulation*: 147–56. ACM, New York, NY, USA. 1981. Also available at `http://doi.acm.Org/10.1145/800209.806466`.

- Stallman, Richard M. *Gnu Emacs Manual: For Version 24.3*. Free Software Foundation, 17th edition. 2013.

- VirtualBox.org. Accessed September 3, 2014. `https://www.virtualbox.org/`.

Chapter 2

- Adafruit Industries. "Adafruit's BeagleBone IO Python Library". Accessed September 3, 2014. `https://github.com/adafruit/adafruit-beaglebone-io-python`.

- Appelbaum, Jacob and Nick Mathewson. *Pluggable transports for circumvention*. 2010. Accessed September 3, 2014. `https://gitweb.torproject.org/torspec.git/blob/refs/heads/master:/proposals/180-pluggable-transport.txt`.

- Dingledine, Roger. "Yes, we know about the Guardian article.". Accessed September 3, 2014. `https://blog.torproject.org/blog/yes-we-know-about-guardian-article`. 2013.

- Dingledine, Roger and Nick Mathewson. *Design of a blocking-resistant anonymity system*. Technical Report 2006-11-001, The Tor Project, `https://research.torproject.org/techreports/blocking-2006-11.pdf`. November 2006.

- Dingledine, Roger, Nick Mathewson, and Paul Syverson. "In Proceedings of the 13th Conference on USENIX Security Symposium - Volume 13, SSYM'04." *Tor: The second-generation onion router*: 21. USENIX Association. Berkeley, CA, USA. 2004. `http://dl.acm.org/citation.cfm?id=1251375.1251396`.

- Electronic Frontier Foundation. "The Legal FAQ for Tor Relay Operators." Accessed September 3, 2014. `https://www.torproject.org/eff/tor-legal-faq.html.en`. 2014

- Fuss, Juergen, Tobias Pulls, and Philipp Winter. "Scramblesuit: a polymorphic network protocol to circumvent censorship." *Proceedings of the 12th ACM workshop on Workshop on Privacy in the electronic society, WPES'13*: 213-24. New York, NY, USA: ACM. 2013. Also available at `http://doi.acm.org/10.1145/2517840.2517856`.

- Grusin, Mike. "Serial LCD quickstart." Accessed September 3, 2014. `https://www.sparkfun.com/tutorials/246`. 2011.

- Kadianakis, George. "New obfsproxy transport: scramblesuit." Accessed September 3, 2014. `https://lists.torproject.org/pipermail/tor-relays/2014-February/003886.html`. 2014

- speedtest-cli. Accessed September 3, 2014. `https://github.com/sivel/speedtest-cli`.

- Tails. Accessed September 3, 2014. `https://tails.boum.org/`.

- Tor Atlas. Accessed September 3, 2014. `https://atlas.torproject.org/`.

- Tor Globe. Accessed September 3, 2014. `https://globe.torproject.org/`.

- Tor Metrics. "Directly connecting users from Turkey." Accessed September 3, 2014. `https://metrics.torproject.org/users.html?graph=userstats-relay-country&start=2014-01-04&end=2014-04-04&country=tr&events=off#userstats-relay-country`.

- Tor Project. "Installing Tor on Debian/Ubuntu." Accessed September 3, 2014. `https://www.torproject.org/docs/debian`.

- Tor Project. *Tc: A Tor control protocol (Version 1)*. Accessed September 3, 2014. `https://gitweb.torproject.org/torspec.git?a=blob_plain;hb=HEAD;f=control-spec.txt`.

- Tor Stem. Accessed September 3, 2014. `https://stem.torproject.org/`.

- Tor Stem. "Tutorials." Accessed September 3, 2014. `https://stem.torproject.org/tutorials.html`.

Chapter 3

- Atmel. "ATAES 132." Accessed September 3, 2014. `http://www.atmel.com/devices/ataes132.aspx`.

- Beagleboard forum. Accessed September 3, 2014. `https://groups.google.com/forum/#!forum/beagleboard`.

- eLinux Wiki. "BeagleBone Black." Accessed September 3, 2014. `http://elinux.org/Beagleboard:BeagleBoneBlack`.

- Chaos Computer Club. "Chaos Computer Club Breaks Apple TouchID." Accessed September 3, 2014. `http://www.ccc.de/en/updates/2013/ccc-breaks-apple-touchid`. 2013.

- Datko, Josh. "BeagleBone Black ATmega Flasher." Accessed September 3, 2014. `https://github.com/jbdatko/BBB_ATmega328P_flasher`. 2014.

- Datko, Josh. "Cryptotronix:CryptoCape." Accessed September 3, 2014. `http://elinux.org/Cryptotronix:CryptoCape`. 2014.

- Datko, Josh. "CryptoCape Device Tree Source." Accessed September 3, 2014. `https://github.com/beagleboard/linux/blob/3.8/firmware/capes/BB-BONE-CRYPTO-00A0.dts`. 2014.

- Datko, Josh. "EClet" Accessed September 3, 2014. `https://github.com/cryptotronix/eclet`. 2014

- Datko, Josh. "Hashlet." Accessed September 3, 2014. `https://github.com/cryptotronix/hashlet`. 2014.

- Electronic Frontier Foundation. "Https Everywhere." Accessed September 3, 2014. `https://www.eff.org/https-everywhere`. 2014.

- Gellesaug, David and Nicole Perlroth. "Russian hackers amass over a billion internet passwords. New York Times." `http://www.nytimes.com/2014/08/06/technology/russian-gang-said-to-amass-more-than-a-billion-stolen-internet-credentials.html`. 2014.

- Texas Instrument. "AM335x Crypto Performance." Accessed September 3, 2014. `http://processors.wiki.ti.com/index.php/AM335x_Crypto_Performance`.

- Munroe, Randall. "Heartbleed explanation." Accessed September 3, 2014. `https://xkcd.com/1354/`. 2014.

- MythBusters. "Crimes and Myth-Demeanors 2." Episode 59. Accessed September 3, 2014. `https://www.youtube.com/watch?v=3Hji3kp_i9k`. 2006

- NXP Semiconductor. *I2C-Bus Specification and User Manual.* `http://www.nxp.com/documents/user_manual/UM10204.pdf`. 2014.

- O'Flynn, Colin. "Clock Glitch Attack Examples - Bypassing Password Check." Accessed September 3, 2014. `https://www.youtube.com/watch?v=Ruphw98JWE&list=UUqc9MJwX_R1pQC6A353JmJg`. 2014.

- Oliveira, David. "BeagleBone Cape EEPROM Generator." Accessed September 3, 2014. `https://github.com/picoflamingo/BBCape_EEPROM`. 2013.

- Petazzoni, Thomas. "Device Tree for Dummies." Embedded Linux Conference Europe. `https://www.youtube.com/watch?v=m_NyYEBxfn8`. 2013.

- Skorobogatov, Dr Sergei. *Physical Attacks on Tamper Resistance: Progress and Lessons*. 2nd ARO Special Workshop on Hardware Assurance. `http://www.cl.cam.ac.uk/~sps32/ARO_2011.pdf`. 2011.

Chapter 4

- Appelbaum, Jacob. "GPG Configuration." Accessed September 3, 2014. `https://github.com/ioerror/duraconf/raw/master/configs/gnupg/gpg.conf`.

- Appelbaum, Jacob, Joseph A. Calandrino, William Clarkson, Edward W. Felten, Ariel J. Feldman, J. Alex Halderman, Nadia Heninger, Seth D. Schoen, and William Paul. *Lest We Remember: Cold-boot Attacks on Encryption Keys*. 52(5): 91-98. Commun. ACM. 2009. Also available at `http://doi.acm.org/10.1145/1506409.1506429`.

- Borisov, Nikita, George Danezis, and Ian Goldberg. DP5: *A Private Presence Service*. Technical Report 2014-10. The Tor Project. `http://cacr.uwaterloo.ca/techreports/2014/cacr2014-10.pdf`. 2014.

- Datko, Josh. "CryptoCape Trusted Platform Module." Accessed September 3, 2014. `http://cryptotronix.com/cryptocape-tpm/`. 2014.

- Free Software Foundation. "Email Self-Defense." Accessed September 3, 2014. `https://emailselfdefense.fsf.org/en/index.html`. 2014.

- Free Software Foundation. *The GNU Privacy Handbook*. `https://www.gnupg.org/gph/en/manual.html`. 1999.

- Greenwald, Glenn. *No Place to Hide: Edward Snowden, the NSA, and the U.S. Surveillance State*. 2014. Metropolitan Books. USA.

- Gutmann, Peter. "An Open-Source Cryptographic Coprocessor." *Proceedings of the 9th Conference on USENIX Security Symposium - Volume 9, SSYM'00*: 8-8. USENIX Association, Berkeley, CA, USA. 2000. Also available at `http://dl.acm.org/citation.cfm?id=1251306.1251314`.

- HAVEGE. Accessed September 3, 2014. `http://www.irisa.fr/caps/projects/hipsor/`.

- Huang, Bunnie. "On Hacking MicroSD Cards." Accessed September 3, 2014. `http://www.bunniestudios.com/blog/?p=3554`. 2013.

- Langner, Ralph. *Stuxnet: Dissecting a Cyberwarfare Weapon*. 9(3): 49-51. IEEE Security and Privacy. 2011. Also available at `http://dx.doi.org/10.1109/MSP.2011.67`.

- Levy, Steven. *Crypto: How the Code Rebels Beat the Government: Saving Privacy in the Digital Age.* Penguin USA, New York, NY, USA. 2001.

- Marlinspike, Moxie. "A Critique of Lavabit." Accessed September 3, 2014. `http://www.thoughtcrime.org/blog/lavabit-critique/`. 2013.

- Microsoft. "United States' Malware Infection Rate More than Doubles in the First Half of 2013." Accessed September 3, 2014. `http://blogs.technet.com/b/security/archive/2014/03/31/united-states-malware-infection-rate-more-than-doubles-in-the-first-half-of-2013.aspx`. 2014.

- National Archives. "Frequently Asked Questions About Optical Storage Media." Accessed September 3, 2014. `http://www.archives.gov/records-mgmt/initiatives/temp-opmedia-faq.html`.

- Opsahl, Kurt. "Why Metadata Matters." Accessed September 3, 2014. `https://www.eff.org/deeplinks/2013/06/why-metadata-matters`.

- riseup.net. "OpenPGP Best Practices." Accessed September 3, 2014. `https://help.riseup.net/en/security/message-security/openpgp/best-practices`.

- Shirey, R. "Internet Security Glossary. RFC 4949 (Informational)." Accessed September 3, 2014. `http://www.ietf.org/rfc/rfc4949.txt`. 2007.

- Trusted Computing Group. "TPM 1.2 Specification." Accessed September 3, 2014. `http://www.trustedcomputinggroup.org/resources/tpm_main_specification`. 2011.

- Tygar, J. D. and Alma Whitten. "Why Johnny can't encrypt: A Usability Evaluation of PGP 5.0." *Proceedings of the 8th Conference on USENIX Security Symposium - Volume 8, SSYM'99*: 14-14. USENIX Association Berkeley, CA, USA. 1999. Also available at `http://dl.acm.org/citation.cfm?id=1251421.1251435`.

- Zimmermann, Philip R. *PGP Source Code and Internals.* MIT Press, Cambridge, MA, USA. 1995.

- Zimmermann, Philip R. *The Official PGP User's Guide.* MIT Press, Cambridge, MA, USA. 1995.

Chapter 5

- Alexander, Chris and Ian Goldberg. "Improved User authentication in Off-the-Record Messaging." *Proceedings of the 2007 ACM Workshop on Privacy in Electronic Society, WPES '07*: 41-47, New York, NY, USA. ACM. 2007. Also available at http://doi.acm.org/10.1145/1314333.1314340.

- Borisov, Nikita, Eric Brewer, and Ian Goldberg. "Off-the-Record Communication, or, Why not to use PGP." *Proceedings of the 2004 ACM Workshop on Privacy in the Electronic Society, WPES '04*: 77-84, New York, NY, USA. ACM 2004. Also available at http://doi.acm.org/10.1145/1029179.1029200.

- Cruise, Brit. "Walkthrough of Diffie-Gellman Key Exchange." Accessed September 3, 2014. https://www.khanacademy.org/computing/computer-science/cryptography/modern-crypt/v/diffie-hellman-key-exchange-part-2.

- EggHEADS.ORG. "Eggdrop." Accessed September 3, 2014. http://www.eggheads.org/.

- EmacsWiki. "ERC Basics." Accessed September 3, 2014. http://www.emacswiki.org/emacs/ErcBasics.

- fellowship. "Join FSFE's Community." Accessed September 3, 2014. https://fsfe.org/fellowship/index.en.html.

- Google. "What is Google Talk?." Accessed September 3, 2014. https://developers.google.com/talk/. 2013.

- Gutmann, Peter. *Everything you Never Wanted to Know about PKI but were Forced to Find Out*. Accessed September 3, 2014. https://www.cs.auckland.ac.nz/~pgut001/pubs/pkitutorial.pdf.

- Hill, Benjamin. "Google has Most of my Email Because it Has All of Yours." Accessed September 3, 2014. http://mako.cc/copyrighteous/google-has-most-of-my-email-because-it-has-all-of-yours. 2014.

- IRC Help. "An IRC Tutorial." Accessed September 3, 2014. http://www.irchelp.org/irchelp/irctutorial.html.

- irssi. "Irssi IRC Client." Accessed September 3, 2014. http://www.irssi.org/.

- Khan Academy. "XOR Bitwise Operation." Accessed September 3, 2014 https://www.khanacademy.org/computing/computer-science/cryptography/ciphers/a/xor-bitwise-operation.

- OAuth. Accessed September 3, 2014. `http://oauth.net/`.

- Rasata, Jeanne. Free Software Foundation. "Associate Member Benefits." Accessed September 3, 2014. `https://www.fsf.org/associate/benefits`. 2012.

- ZNC Wiki. "ZNC." Accessed September 3, 2014. `http://wiki.znc.in/ZNC`.

Index

W

Web-of-Trust, GPG Privacy Handbook
  reference 87

X

xkcd comic
  URL 53

Z

zero-knowledge proof 111
ZNC
  connecting, from IRC client 123
  networks, adding to 121, 122
  OTR connections, establishing
    through 124, 125
ZNC configuration
  used, for managing IRC connections 116
ZNC server
  OTR, adding to 120

Thank you for buying
BeagleBone for Secret Agents

About Packt Publishing

Packt, pronounced 'packed', published its first book "*Mastering phpMyAdmin for Effective MySQL Management*" in April 2004 and subsequently continued to specialize in publishing highly focused books on specific technologies and solutions.

Our books and publications share the experiences of your fellow IT professionals in adapting and customizing today's systems, applications, and frameworks. Our solution based books give you the knowledge and power to customize the software and technologies you're using to get the job done. Packt books are more specific and less general than the IT books you have seen in the past. Our unique business model allows us to bring you more focused information, giving you more of what you need to know, and less of what you don't.

Packt is a modern, yet unique publishing company, which focuses on producing quality, cutting-edge books for communities of developers, administrators, and newbies alike. For more information, please visit our website: www.packtpub.com.

About Packt Open Source

In 2010, Packt launched two new brands, Packt Open Source and Packt Enterprise, in order to continue its focus on specialization. This book is part of the Packt Open Source brand, home to books published on software built around Open Source licenses, and offering information to anybody from advanced developers to budding web designers. The Open Source brand also runs Packt's Open Source Royalty Scheme, by which Packt gives a royalty to each Open Source project about whose software a book is sold.

Writing for Packt

We welcome all inquiries from people who are interested in authoring. Book proposals should be sent to author@packtpub.com. If your book idea is still at an early stage and you would like to discuss it first before writing a formal book proposal, contact us; one of our commissioning editors will get in touch with you.

We're not just looking for published authors; if you have strong technical skills but no writing experience, our experienced editors can help you develop a writing career, or simply get some additional reward for your expertise.

BeagleBone Home Automation

ISBN: 978-1-78328-573-0   Paperback: 178 pages

Live your sophisticated dream with home automation using BeagleBone

1. Practical approach to home automation using BeagleBone; starting from the very basics of GPIO control and progressing up to building a complete home automation solution.

2. Covers the operating principles of a range of useful environment sensors, including their programming and integration to the server application.

Building a Home Security System with BeagleBone

ISBN: 978-1-78355-960-2   Paperback: 120 pages

Build your own high-tech alarm system at a fraction of the cost

1. Build your own state-of-the-art security system.

2. Monitor your system from any place where you can receive e-mails.

3. Add control of other systems such as sprinklers and gates.

Please check **www.PacktPub.com** for information on our titles

Raspberry Pi for Secret Agents

ISBN: 978-1-84969-578-7   Paperback: 152 pages

Turn your Raspberry Pi into your very own secret agent toolbox with this set of exciting projects!

1. Detect an intruder on camera and set off an alarm.

2. Listen in or record conversations from a distance.

3. Find out what the other computers on your network are up to.

Rapid BeagleBoard Prototyping with MATLAB and Simulink

ISBN: 978-1-84969-604-3   Paperback: 152 pages

Leverage the power of BeagleBoard to develop and deploy practical embedded projects

1. Develop and validate your own embedded audio/video applications rapidly with Beagleboard.

2. Create embedded Linux applications on a pure Windows PC.

3. Full of illustrations, diagrams, and tips for rapid BeagleBoard Prototyping with clear, step-by-step instructions and hands-on examples.

Please check **www.PacktPub.com** for information on our titles

www.ingramcontent.com/pod-product-compliance
Lightning Source LLC
LaVergne TN
LVHW081344050326
832903LV00024B/1312